숨 쉬는 옹기,
그 멋에 끌리다

Respiring Onggi Object of Admiration

김덕신 그리고 쓰다
Written and illustrated by Kim Duk Shin

초판 발행 2023년 10월 9일 | 글 그림 김덕신 | 번역 김윤정 | 펴낸이 안창현 | 펴낸곳 코드미디어
북 디자인 Micky Ahn | 교정 교열 민혜정 | ISBN 979-11-93355-02-2 (03810)

등록 2001년 3월 7일 등록번호 제 25100-2001-5호 | 주소 서울시 은평구 갈현로 318-1, 1층 | 전화 02-6326-1402
팩스 02-388-1302 | 전자우편 codmedia@codmedia.com | 정가 15,000원

들어가기에 앞서

  1974년 미국 미주리 주립대 도서관에서 일한 적이 있었는데 어느 날, 엘리베이터에서 한 미국 교수가 대뜸 '한국의 금속활자가 요하네스 구텐베르크의 금속활자보다 얼마만큼 앞섰는지 아시나요?'라고 내게 물은 적이 있었다. 이때 1377년 충북 청주 흥덕사에서 금속 활자로 간행된 『직지심체요절』이 독일의 성경보다 78년이나 앞선 인쇄본인 것과 그러한 금속활자의 기술을 발전시킨 역사의 후손으로서의 '자부심'*을 제대로 말하지 못했었기에 이후 우리의 것에 더 많은 관심을 가지게 되었고 이 마음이 이어져 1977년에 한국으로 돌아와 옹기를 모으게 되었으며 지금 이 책을 쓰게 된 계기가 되었다.

  신이 흙으로 사람을 빚으셨다는 기독교의 인류사와 사람이 흙으로 그릇을 빚어 구워 사용한 도자사가 맞물려 가는 것을 볼 때 인류의 역사가 도자기의 역사라 해도 과언이 아닌 듯하다. 한국의 도기와 질그릇의 보존이 폭 넓은 연구의 시발점이 됐었다.

---

* 한국에서 인쇄된 가장 오래된 책인 『직지심체요절』은 독일의 구텐베르크 성경(독일, 1455년)보다 78년이나 앞선 인쇄본이다. 1377년 충북 청주 흥덕사에서 금속활자로 간행된 한국의 소중한 문화유산이라는 자부심을 말한다.

그릇의 시작은 옹기이다. 우리 겨레의 기초 자원으로 식문화의 중심적 역할을 해온 그릇으로 옹기는 궁궐의 임금님 장독대에서부터 농가의 부엌 살림에 이르기까지 만백성이 사용하였던 겨레의 그릇이다.

우리나라 도자사에서 옹기(도기)는 신석기 시대의 연질토기에서 경질토기, 통일신라 말기에는 고화도 회유옹기로 발전되어 왔다. 이 과정에서 고려초기에는 녹유청자의 생산기술을 터득하는 기반이 되었고 고려 중기 비색 청자와 조선 백자의 뿌리 역할을 하며 자기 계통과 더불어 도기라는 양대 주류를 형성하며 지금에 이르게 된 것이다. 옹기는 한반도 그릇이자 문화 효시이며 근간이 된다고 할 수 있는 것이다.

이 책은 이러한 옹기를 통하여 정성과 사랑으로 생활을 아름답게 가꾸어 왔던 조상들의 멋과 맛의 지혜를, 오늘을 사는 우리와 내일을 살아야 할 후손들에게 전하고 싶은 마음에서 탄생하였다.

고구려 여인이 용두레로 살던 집.
우물에서 물을 긷는다. 우물 가장자리에 크고 작은 물 항아리가 놓여있다.
(고구려 276년 경 황해도 안악의 제3호분 벽화의 한 장면)

머리말

숨 쉬는 옹기甕器

사람들이 '옹기'라고 하면 장독대에 놓였던 큰 독과 항아리들을 먼저 생각한다. 우리 민족이 옹기의 전신인 토기를 사용했던 모습은 삼국시대 고구려 고분 벽화 속 부엌 장면이나 우물가의 여인들 모습에서 볼 수 있다. 조선조에 와서는 옹기가 어떻게 만들어졌는지부터, 날 옹기를 굽던 불 가마터, 그리고 구워진 옹기를 지게에 잔뜩 지고 가는 옹기장수 등을 묘사한 서민 생활상 및 궁중 생활을 보여주는 조선후기 그림 등을 통해서 옹기의 역사를 파악할 수 있다.

수천 년 전부터 오늘에 이르기까지 똑같은 도기를 사용하고 있는 민족이 세계에 또 있을까 싶은 한국만의 세계 유일한 옹기 문화는, 주택에서 아파트로 변화한 주거문화와 함께 달라진 식문화 등이 서로 맞물리며 우리 주변에서 점점 자취를 감추고 있는 형세다.

나와 옹기 사이의 인연은 퍽 오래전부터다. 피곤하고 지쳐있을 때 틈을 내어 우리의 옛 물건을 파는 곳을 찾아다니면 그렇게 기분이 좋고 생기가 나곤 했다. 그곳에서는 눈으로 보는 것뿐 아니고 손으로 직접 만져볼 수 있어서 좋았고 나아가 우리 것의 아름다움과 멋에 흠뻑 취할 수 있었다. 옹기의 다양한 종

십자가 연가

Nov. 28 '20 송

류와 이름, 쓰임새, 어느 지방 것인가를 묻고 대화하며 많은 것을 배우고 알고 느낄 수 있어서 유익했던 어느 날 한 상점의 주인으로부터 아주 독특한 굴뚝의 연가煙家를 선물 받았는데 이 연가 덕분에 우리 것에 대한 관심은 더욱 커졌다. 아직도 이 연가와 비슷한 연가를 보지 못했다.

옹기에 대해 더 알고 싶어서 박물관 도서 자료실도 가고, 영상 자료실이나 헌책방 등을 다니면서 스크랩도 하고, 지방에 가서 사진도 찍었다. 지방 사람들이 도시로 떠나면서 빈 농가 뜰에 덩그러니 남아 있는 깨진 옹기들, 어떤 경우에는 깨져서 뒹굴고 있는 독들을 볼 때면 '조상들이 귀하게 쓰던 것인데…', '다시는 만들기도 쉽지 않은데…' 하며 속상했던 적이 많았다.

옹기는 우리 조상들이 독창적이고 과학적이며 위생적인 방법으로 제작해왔다. 여러 작업 과정을 거쳐 흙을 빚어내어 얼마 동안 건조시킨 후 부엽토의 일종인 약토와 재를 물과 함께 개어 만든 잿물로 옷을 입힌다. 그런 다음 그릇 표면을 손가락이나 나무 조각으로 긁어내 문양을 만드는데 이때 옹기의 문양은 미적 표현은 물론이고 숨구멍을 트여주는 역할과 동시에 옹기마다 고유한 특징을 부여한다. 이러한 우리 조상의 지혜를 감탄하게 된다. 이후 파손되지 않을 정도로 그늘에서 건조되면 햇볕에 건조시켜 '날그릇'이 되었을 때 한 가마분의 양을 햇볕에 다시 건조시킨다. 옹기 가마로 옮겨서 1,200°C 내외의 고온에서 10일 동안 구워낸 그릇이 옹기인데, 이 과정에서 점토질과 모래 알갱이가 고열에 의해 이완되면서 그릇 표면 전체에 미세한 숨구멍이 생김으로써 숨 쉬는 옹기가 태어나는 것이다. 이렇게 다 구운 옹기를 두드리면 독특한 맑은 소리가 나고, 옹기 뚜껑은 마치 무쇠처럼 무겁고 단단하다.

우리 식품인 간장, 된장, 고추장, 젓갈 등을 숨 쉬는 옹기에 담아 발효시키고 저장·보관해서 한 해의 양식으로 준비하여 푸근하고 풍요롭고 넉넉한 마음으로 살아간다. 여름에는 장독 안에서 불순물이 밖으로 끈적끈적하게 나와 우리의 어머니, 할머니들은 아침과 저녁 하루 두 번씩 독들을 닦아줌으로써 독이 계속 호흡할 수 있도록 해주었다. 반들반들한 장독대는 주부들에게 부지런함의 상징이며 은근한 자랑이었다.

숨 쉬는 옹기는 지역의 기후와 자연 환경에 따라, 그리고 쓰임새와 만드는 사람에 따라 각각 특색이 있는 독특한 형태를 갖추고 있다. 이러한 사례 중 하나로 조선 후기에 천주교 박해 당시 신자들이 산 속에 숨어들어가 호구지책으로 옹기를 구우면서 십자가나 '익투스(물고기)' 문양*을 옹기에 그려 넣어 하나님이 살아 계심을 나타냈다.

---

* 그리스어로 익투스는 하나님의 아들 '구세주 예수그리스도'를 뜻하는 그리스어의 첫 글자에서 따온 단어이며 그리스어로 같은 발음의 '익투스'는 물고기를 말한다.

숨 쉬는 옹기는 흙으로 빚은 것이기에 천연에 가까워 무해·무독하고 조심스럽게 쓰면 수십 년 내지 수천 년까지도 거뜬히 쓸 수 있으나 파손되었을 경우 자연으로의 토화土化 현상이 빨라 자연의 흙으로 돌아가니 요즘의 심각한 환경오염 걱정도 없는 첨단의 재질을 갖고 있음이 또한 자랑거리다. 그러나 일제강점기 시절 연료 절약을 이유로 낮은 온도에 굽는데다, 유약에 화학약품인 광명단을 섞어 윤기는 나지만 광명단의 납 성분 때문에 그릇에 담긴 음식물에 독소가 들어가고 옹기의 숨구멍을 막아 음식이 자연스럽게 발효되는 것을 방해했다. 이 기간 거치며 전통 옹기를 만드는 장인들은 대부분 몰락해 버리고 자랑스러웠던 숨 쉬는 옹기는 스테인리스와 플라스틱 그릇에 밀려 명맥이 거의 끊어지게 되었다. 가장 전통적인 것이 가장 세계적이라는 말을 떠올리며, 우리의 숨 쉬는 옹기를 아끼고 우수함을 알리는 데 모두 앞장섰으면 하는 마음이다.

옹기는 점토를 채취해 가마에 굽는 동안 일천 번의 손길과 눈길로 정성을 다해야 세상에 모습을 드러내는 그릇이다. 전통적이고, 과학적인 옹기가 우리 민족과 함께한 유구한 역사가 오늘까지 가닿은 것은 '숨 쉬는 옹기'가 유일하다.

1991년 5월 옹기장이가 중요 무형 문화재로 규정되었고, 2013년에는 김장 문화가 유네스코 세계무형문화유산으로 등재

됐다. 그러나 흙과 땀과 정성으로 태어난 '숨 쉬는 옹기'는 세계 무형문화유산에 아직 등재되지 못한 상태다.

이 책의 집필 목적은 두 가지다. 첫 번째는 우리 민족의 유구한 역사와 함께해온, 전통적이고 과학적인 숨 쉬는 옹기가 세계무형문화유산에 등재되어야 할 마땅한 이유를 널리 알리고자 함이다. 두 번째는 그 독특한 소박미가 아름다워 예술적이기도 한 우리의 숨 쉬는 옹기를, 지금의 주거문화 및 식문화 변화로 우리 곁에서 사라져 가는 안타까움과 우리 것의 소중함과 아름다움을 깨닫지 못하고 있음을 많은 사람들이 알아주길 바라는 마음 때문이다.

숨 쉬는 옹기는 우리만의 것이 아닌 인류 자산이며 문화유산이다. 전통 옹기는 넉넉함과 포용감, 무엇을 담고 있어도 드러나지 않는 여백의 아름다움으로 우리 곁에 있다. 무의식의 아름다움과 소중함을 일깨워 준다.

옹기는 소성이 가장 힘들고 중요하다. 그 중에서도 가장 큰 노력은 가마 온도 맞추기다. 1,210°C에서는 웬만하면 깨지지 않는 강도를 지닌 옹기가 만들어진다. 장작불로 10일 동안 구워내 진짜 솜씨꾼의 솜씨로 만들어진 옹기를 사용해 만든 음식은 맛도 좋고, 건강에도 한몫한다.

정성이 장맛이다.

질 좋은 콩으로 만든 간장과 된장은 무색소, 무조미료, 무방부제이며 마음이 오덕, 정성이 오덕, 그리고 장이 오덕이다. 오덕은 다른 맛과 섞어도 제맛을 낸다는 단심이고, 오랫동안 상하지 않는다는 항심이며, 비리고 기름진 냄새 제거하는 불심이다. 매운맛을 부드럽게 하는 선심이고, 어떤 음식과도 조화 이룬다는 화심이다.

좋은 장을 담그기 위해서는 늦가을 콩을 너무 과숙하지 말아야 하고 콩을 삶아 콩의 7할 정도가 파쇄되도록 절구질하여 메주를 만들고 이를 빚어서 꾸덕꾸덕해지면 짚으로 매달아 월동한다. 이 기간에 발효균이 들어앉아 포자를 터트리는데 옛 어머니들은 이를 보고 메주에 꽃이 핀다고 했다. 해동이 되면 음력 정월 첫 말일을 길일로 여겨 전통 장을 담근다.

짚불로 잘 소독된 항아리에 메주를 넣고 소금물을 부어 항아리의 7부 능선까지 오르도록 채우고, 메주가 소금물 위로 떠오르지 못하게 대나무 살을 꽂아 누름 역할을 하게 하였다.

장맛이 변하지 않도록 소금물 위에 붉은 고추와 숯 그리고 대추를 함께 띄운다. 고추는 매운 맛을 더하는 역할이고 유해균 침입을 방지해주는 숯은 정화의 목적이고, 대추는 간장의 단맛을 냄과 동시에 붉은색을 강화하여 액막이를 하고자 했던 것이다. 금줄(일반 새끼줄과 다르게 왼손으로 꼬아서 만든 것)에 숯, 고추, 솔잎, 창호지를 끼워 느슨하게 둘러치며, 창호지를 버선 모양의 본을 떠서 장항아리의 몸통에 거꾸로 붙이고 해충에 의한 피해를 예방하고자 하였다.

장을 담그는 기본 재료는 물, 소금, 콩이지만 어머니의 정성은 다음날부터 시작된다. 해가 좋은 아침이면 항아리 뚜껑을 열어 소금물을 증발시키고, 해가 기울기 전에 항아리의 뚜껑을 덮는다. 습한 여름 소금물 위에 하얀 골마지가 끼면 걷어내고, 발효 과정에서 항아리 표면에 소금쩍과 골마지가 뒤섞인 때는 연신 닦아 주어야 한다. 이렇게 정성으로 가꾸며 맛 좋은 장으로 거듭나기를 기원하였다. 이 모든 과정에는 '숨 쉬는 옹기'가 함께한다.

한국의 정체성을 담은 '숨 쉬는 옹기'는 자연스러운 미의 완성이다. 옹기가 아름다움을 뿜어내기까지 쌓인 세월과 정성이 '숨 쉬는 옹기'를 만들었고, 장인 정신을 요하는 전통 기법으로 비로소 완성되었다. 이렇게 최적의 조건을 갖추어 그릇이 숨을 쉬는 구조로 만들어진 신비로운 그릇인 것이다. 한국에 옹기 문화가 태동하지 않았다면 CODEX*에 김치, 된장, 고추장이 등록되는 쾌거를 이룰 수 없었을 것이다.

---

* CODEX : 세계 식품 규격위원회. 전 세계에 통용될 수 있는 기준과 규격을 정해놓은 WTO 산하의 국제 기구.

차례

04 들어가기에 앞서
08 머리말

21 1부. 옹기의 개념
29 2부. 옹기의 선과 문양
39 3부. 전통옹기의 기공, '숨 쉬는 그릇' 옹기
51 4부. 질그릇 예찬
61 5부. 옹기의 세계무형문화유산 등재 이유
71 6부. 북한 옹기

82 감사의 말
90 시 「숨 쉬는 옹기」
95 참고문헌

English translation
97 Respiring Onggi Object of Admiration

통도사 서운암 초입 장독대 앞에 선 성파 스님은 "단독 주택에서 아파트로 주거문화가 바뀌면서 버려졌던 항아리에 전통 된장을 담갔더니 명품이 됐다" "지금 하찮아 보이는 것도 그 가치를 되새겨 봐야 한다"라고 밝혔다.

Standing in front of the jangdokdae at the entrance to Seounam Hermitage at Tongdosa Temple, Buddhist monk Seongpa said, "The traditional soybean paste that was fermented in the discarded onggi jars as the housing culture changed from a single-family house to apartments, became a luxury item. Even things that seem insignificant now, their value must be pondered upon."

1

옹기의 개념

옹기는 대다수의 국내 학자들뿐 아니라 세계의 전문가들 사이에서도 중요한 연구 대상이 되어 깊은 관심을 받고 있다. 1987년에 옹기를 연구한 미국인 학자 로버트 세이어스는 옹기의 역사 및 옹기의 개념 정리나 혹은 옹기의 과학적 고찰보다는 인류학적 방법을 따라 연구하여 『한국의 옹기, 항아리』*이라는 책을 발간하기도 하였다. 그는 주로 탐방을 통하여 1970년대의 상황을 조사·분석하여 정리한 내용이다.

이러한 상황은 옹기가 존재하여온 태고 이래의 장구한 세월 중 특정한 시기를 집중 분석한 것에 불과하다. 비록 옹기에 대한 인류학적인 접근이었다고 할 수 있으나 이러한 방식은 자칫 호기심의 측면으로 흘러가 일본인들이 고려청자나 조선백자를 골동품으로 취급했던 것과 유사한 흐름 속으로 빠져들 수 있다. 옹기에 대한 논의가 그 업적을 충분히 축적하지 못한 상황에서 흐름이 왜곡되면 도자사에서 우리가 느끼는 혼란이 옹기에서도 야기될 가능성이 존재하게 된다. 이러한 경향이 관공서나 궁중에도 파급되어 옹기라는 단어를 도기와 서슴없이 혼용하게 되었다.

---

* 1987년 Smithsonian Institution Press에서 출간한 『The Korean Onggi, Potter』 참조.

옹기가 토기를 망라한 것이고 그 질그릇이 태고 이래로 만들어져 오는 것이라고 한다면, 옹기 그것은 우리나라 도자사에 근간을 이루는 바로 골격 그 자체라고 할 수 있다.

질그릇에 의도적으로 유약을 입히기 시작 한 것은 최근이었다고 알려져 있다. 옹기의 태반은 질그릇이었고 옻그릇은 그 수에 비할 때 극히 제한된 것이라고 할 수 있다. 우리만의 옹기는 질그릇, 오지그릇을 통칭하는 포괄적인 용어로 쓰이기도 하고 큰 독을 지칭하는 좁은 의미의 단어로 사용되기도 한다.

유약을 입히지 않고 굽는 것을 질그릇이라 하고 유약을 입혀 굽는 것을 옻그릇이라 한다. 이러한 옻그릇을 오지그릇이라 부르기 시작하였고, 오지그릇이 보편화 되면서 옹기라는 단어가 유행하고 그 옹기는 유약을 입힌 독이 기본이 되는 듯 알려지고 있다. 옹기를 굽는 사람들은 소성 방법에 따라 질그릇(질독), 푸레독, 반오지, 오지 등으로 구분한다.

질그릇을 구울 때 그을음을 먹여 질의 색이 검은 회색으로 나타나며 이때 연기(煙)를 먹은 그릇에 방수 기능이 더해진다.

푸레독은 질그릇과 같은 방법으로 연기를 먹여서 굽지만 가마 안의 온도가 상승하여 질이 유용될 즈음에 소금을 뿌려 넣는다. 이 일을 도공들은 "소금을 친다"라고 하는데 소금을 적게 혹은 많이 치는 것에 따라 표면의 윤택이 달라진다.

푸레독의 존재는 소금을 치지 않고 굽던 시절의 질그릇과는 단계를 달리하고 있음을 알게 된다.

반오지의 소성법은 소금 치는 기법을 따르나 푸레독처럼 연기를 먹이지 않고 질의 소성된 본색을 그대로 드러내게 한다. 완성되었을 때에 표면은 유약을 입힌 듯이 윤색되어 오지그릇과 같은 효과를 갖는다. 그러나 유약을 입힌 오지그릇과는 분명히 다르다.

오지(옻그릇)라는 개념은 그릇에 유약을 입혀 그 유약이 용융되었을 때에 윤택을 채택한 것이다. 옻그릇은 오지그릇이라 부르고, 오지그릇이 보편화되면서 옹기라는 단어가 유행되고 그 옹기는 석간주에서 더 보완된 유약을 입힌 독이 기본이 되는 것으로 알려지고 있다.

오늘날 옹기라는 개념이 이러한 과정을 거치며 완성되었던 것이다. 옻그릇이 완성되기 이전 단계의 것을 반오지라 하는데 반오지는 푸레독과 다르고 오지그릇과도 다른 기법으로 조성된다.

시루와 장군
시루는 떡·쌀 등을 찌는 데 쓰는 질그릇이고, 장군은 물·술·간장 등을 옮길 때 사용하는 오지 그릇으로 배에 아가리가 있는 것이 특징이다.

Siru and Janggun
A siru is an earthenware vessel (jilgeureut) used when steaming rice cakes or rice, and a janggun is a vessel (ojigeureut) designed to transport water, liquor, soy sauce, and so on, and there is a mouth on the belly of the vessel.

앞에서 독의 조성과 소성기법에 따른 차이를 정리해 보았는데 중요한 사실은 오지그릇만의 옹기와는 그 내용에 현격한 차이가 있음을 알게 된다.

옹기는 지역에 따라 고유한 특색을 지니고 있어서, 지역적 특징 탐색에 유용하게 활용될 수 있다. 각 시대에 따른 토기의 특성이 있어 문화성을 이해할 수 있는 역사 인식과 연계되는 것이므로 옹기는 민족의 문화유산으로 중요시해야 마땅하다.

문제는 옹기를 수호하는 대책이 국가적인 배려와 인식이 있어야 성과를 거둘 수 있다는 것이다. 대단히 많은 양의 옹기가 해외로 유출되고 있는 것은 그들의 안목에 옹기가 중요하다는 인식이 있는 것이므로 그를 이용하여 토산품으로 만들어 팔면, 옛것을 보호하고 새로운 것을 세계에 보급하는 방안이 강구될 것이다. 국가에서도 크게 장려할 만하고 덕수궁에서 열린 옹기 전람회를 계기로 옹기의 중요성을 진작하고 선양하는 방편도 수립되기를 기대한다.

진주 어느 길을 걷다가 만난 옹기 화분.
While walking along the street in Jinju I stumbled upon a flower pot artwork, the broken onggi transformed into a splendid flower pot.

2

옹기의 선과 문양

항아리의 곡선은 물레의 회전에 의한 대칭적인 구조로써 자연스럽고 세련된 미적 감각이 드러나지 않은 순박함과 친근한 곡선미를 지니고 있다. 한국의 옹기는 이러한 특징와 함께 담백하고 유연하며 아름다움, 즉 관조의 미를 지니고 있다. 경사에 따른 완만함은 무늬들과 잘 조화되어 그 조형적 아름다움까지 더해지는 것이다.

몸의 율동과 손놀림의 궤적에서 나오는 선의 아름다움과 옹기 문양에 나타나는 파곡선의 반복은 비대칭 성격을 띠고 있거니와 축소 또는 팽창되는 파곡선의 곡선은 그 뿌리가 정원正圓에서부터 파생됨을 알 수 있다.

만다라의 해석

스위스의 심리학자 융*이 제시한 만다라의 세계와 한국의 옹기 문양에서 동일하게 나타나는 방사선형의 정상 부분은 '집단의식에서 솟아오르는 산山으로서의 새로운 세계'를 상징한다. 의식적인 상징으로 태양은 산정山頂을 형성한다는 것. 다시 말

---

* 칼 구스타프 융(Carl Gustav Jung, 1875~1961) : 스위스의 정신의학자로 분석심리학의 개척자. 만다라에 심리학적 의미를 부여하고 이를 치료 분야에 적용하였다.

수저통 | 유약을 긁어내는 박지기법을 사용했다.
Cutlery Holder | Using the technique of scraping off the glaze.

하면 자연의 운행 법칙과 인간 심상의 흐름이 동일한 주·객 패턴에서 형성·분화됨을 알 수 있다. 이는 단적으로 옹기 문양의 잡초와 곡식 모양으로 나타나는 독장이의 유토피아적 생명의 발현이 현실의 암담함을 떠나 조형의 원초적 에너지를 통한 리비도 행위 즉 흔적, 자취, 상징으로 나타낸 것이 1900년을 전후하여 한반도에서 발현된 옹기 문양의 본질이라고 보는 것이다.

태극으로서의 해석

힘의 가장 원초적 상징은 태극 모양이라는 것. 칼 구스타프 융에 의하면 조형 세계에 있어 가장 개념적 재현을 잘 이해해 주는 것이 동양의 태극Tao이다. 이러한 옹기 문양 세계들은 '태극'이 상징하는 바로서 기억되어질 것이 분명하다. 강화도에서 발견된 옹기 장인이 그린 것으로 보이는 '문양', '산수 경 관문' 옹기가 결정적 조형 가치이다. 이것을 옹기 문양의 본질이라고 보는 것이다.

A.D 1900년 이전부터 한국인들의 무의식 세계 바탕에는 잘 살고자 하는 인간 원형적 욕구가 옹기와 장독 공간을 통하여 나타났다. 태극으로서의 해석에서 힘의 가장 원초적 상징은 태극 문양이라는 것이고 칼 구스타프 융에 의하면 동양의 태극은 음과 양을 끌어들이는 힘으로 차지하고 있어 시간의 패턴을 유지하고 있다는 것이다.

양각으로 새긴 태극 문양 옹기
옹기 문화가 비록 잠시 부흥되었다 사라져가고 있다 하더라도 옹기에 새겨진 문양이 담고 있는 세계는 태극이 상징하는 바로서 오래도록 기억될 것이 분명하다.

Patriotic Symbol of Taegeuk Embossed on the Pot.
It is certain that the onggi culture, which had a brief revival before it disappeared, will be remembered for a long time as the world of patterns symbolized by Taegeuk.

법칙이 존재하는 +와 −의 결합과, 나아가 음양의 조화로서 소우주에서 미립자에 이르는 일반 조직론의 밑바탕을 이루고 있다. 그 문양 세계들은 오래도록 태극이 상징하는 바로서 기억되어질 것이 분명하다.

미적인 면에서 항아리의 선은 중부 지방보다는 남부 지방 항아리가 큰 곡선으로 나타난다.

또한 항아리는 지역의 기후에 따라 형태적 차이를 나타낸다. 식품 저장은 일조량과 지면 복사열에 의하여 영향을 받는데 항아리의 형태 또한 선조들의 경험에 의한 지혜에서 도출된 모양이라고 볼 수 있을 것이다.

항아리 문양도 각 지방마다 다양하게 표현되었다. 서울의 경우 난초와 나비 등의 구상적 문양을 많이 볼 수 있고 전라도는 파도, 죽엽, 초파 등의 문양이 지배적이다. 이는 옹기 가마의 특성상 다양한 형태의 옹기들이 어느 옹기장이가 만든 것인지를 분별하고 각자의 기호를 항아리에 새기기 시작한 것이 문양으로 발전된 것이라고 볼 수 있다. 또한 소중한 사람이나 특정한 장소에서 사용될 옹기는 주문자의 요구에 부합되는 문양이 각별하게 새겨지기도 했다.

십자가 무늬가 새겨진 옹기
Onggi Hangari with Cross Design

천주교 박해로 십자가 문양이나, 신자 간에 표시로 물고기 (예수님 상징)문양을 은밀하게, 항아리 어깨 위치의 내부 벽면이나 바닥 언저리, 그리고 뚜껑의 안쪽에 추상적인 형식으로 새겨진 경우가 많다.

뚜껑 안쪽에 우물 정#자형이나 나뭇가지 형태로 십자가 긋는 순서대로 좌에서 우로 평행선을 긋고, 위에서 아래로 수직선을 그어 열 십자+로 교차하는 방식으로 그려 넣은 문양을 발견할 수 있다.

항아리의 외부 벽면에 그려진 문양들은 단순히 유약을 벗겨낸 것들이 다수이지만 물고기 문양, 석류 문양, 포도 문양은 음각이나 양각으로, 귀貴하게는 투각透刻하여 새겨 넣은 것도 발견된다.

물고기 문양 단지
물고기란 뜻의 그리스어 '익투스'는 예수, 그리스도, 하나님의 아들, 구세주를 나타낸다. 로마에서 그리스도 박해가 한창일 때 초대 교회 신자들은 의사소통과 신분 확인을 위해 암호의 형태로서 땅이나 지하 무덤(Catacomba) 벽에 물고기 그림을 그려 서로 확인했다고 한다. 출구도 찾기 힘든 곳에서 물고기 머리 향하는 방향따라 집회 장소를 찾았다. 이는 조선의 박해 시대 경우와 흡사하다. 옹기의 벽과 밑바닥에 그려 신앙을 지키려는 노력을 표현했다.

Small Earthenware Pot (Danji) with Fish Design, North Korea
The name "ichthus," which is the Greek word for fish, represents Jesus Christ, the Son of God, and the Savior. During the height of the persecution of Christians in Rome, new Christian believers drew the fish on the ground or on the walls of catacombs as a secret code to communicate or to identify each other. They found the locations of their meetings in a place where it was difficult to find the exit by following the direction the fish's head was facing. The situation was similar to the religious persecution of the Joseon period. The symbols painted on the surface and the bottom of the pottery expressed the believers' deep commitment to the faith.

3

전통 옹기의 기공, '숨 쉬는 그릇' 옹기

우리나라에서 개발한 고유의 식품인 김치 및 각종 발효 식품을 만들 때 사용될 뿐만 아니라 그것을 오래 저장할 수 있는 것이 '숨 쉬는 옹기'다. 지역별로 다른 일조량에 따라 축적된 한국 도예의 기술력과 기능이 높은 수준에 도달하여 세계 도예를 압도한다. 옹기 형태는 일조량과 용도에 따라 지역적 특성을 지니고 있다. 또한 소성燒成 방법 및 지역별 풍토와 관습도 일조량과 더불어 옹기의 형태를 결정짓는 요소로 작용한다.

발효 음식을 장기 보관하여야 하는 한반도의 전통 식문화 특성상 조선의 옹기는 일상생활에 필수적인 저장 용기로서 발전할 수밖에 없는 흐름이었다. 이는 생활에 필요한 도구를 독창적으로 개발해온 한반도 역사의 일부이다.

선사시대 이래 발전해온 토기에 유약칠을 하지 않은 고급 도기, 옹기의 기원은 흙물과 잿물을 조합하여 빚은 후 높은 온도로 소성하는 기술로 시작한다. 전통 도기 제작 기술과 도기 시유 기법을 가장 독창적인 도기인 옹기로 계승되어진다.

옹기는 지극히 현대적인 조형이다. 그러나 이러한 조형적 예술성이나 색감의 중후함과 다양성은 한국의 생활사를 대변하는 민족 자료로서만 인식되어 왔다.

옹기는 불의 조화로 특유의 묘한 색조를 지니고 있다. 이러한 다갈색 옹기는 가장 한국적인 정서를 담고 있고 한국 전통 도자기의 하나이기도 하다. 옹기 문화는 옹기가 이루고 있던 쾌적한 삶의 영위, 살림살이로써의 정서가 가득 담겨 있기에 오래전부터 우리 민족과 함께 존속되어 근원을 이루고 있다.

숨 쉬는 물독에 담긴 끓이지 않은 물을 마셔도 아무 탈이 없었다는 연구 결과를 통해 저절로 깨끗해지는 자정自淨 능력을 지녔음이 과학적으로 밝혀졌다.

나락(볏짚단)으로 옹기를 훑어내는데 이때 사용하는 잘 마른 볏짚에는 '고초균'이 존재하고 있으며 이는 장을 발효하는 과정에 필요한 미생균으로 알려져 있다. 전통 장류의 생산은 무욕의 과학적 행위이다. 장의 주성분은 알칼리성 염류이고 이 염류는 세균을 흡착하며 중화하는 능력이 있다.

음기인 구름과 비, 양기인 태양과 맑은 공기를 통해서 독(옹기)을 이용한 선조들의 발효 과학이 한민족의 장 문화와 함께 한다는 사실은 과학적 근거로 밝혀진 바이다.

붉은 고추는 장독에서 중요한 향신료이다. 고추에 함유된 캡사이신Capsaicin은 살균과 방부 효과가 뛰어난 물질로, 따라서 고추를 장 속에 넣는 것도 과학적 사고의 결과이다. 장독에 붙이던 하얀 버선본에서도 조상의 지혜를 엿볼 수 있다.

스웨덴 과학자들이 2012년에 발표한 내용에 의하면 해충이 가장 싫어하는 색이 흰색이라고 한다. 우리 조상은 버선본을 장독에 붙임으로써 해충을 쫓아낸 것이다. 이렇듯 장독에 숨겨져 있던 과거의 과학이 현대 과학의 힘으로 밝혀지고 있다.

장독에 두른 새끼에 솔잎을 엮어 매달기도 하는데 이는 잡균을 퇴치하는 장독대의 보호수 역할을 해준다. 현대 과학을 통해 밝혀졌듯이, 소나무의 솔잎에는 살균성을 지닌 피톤치드라는 물질이 분비되기 때문이다.

옹기의 완성은 다양한 조건이 조화롭게 맞아떨어져야 한다. 옹기를 만드는 날 옹기 대장의 신바람이 어느 정도냐에 따라 다르고, 질과 약토를 언제 어디에서 캐어 왔느냐에 따라 다르고, 일 년 중 어느 달에 구웠으며 그날 바람은 어떠했느냐에 따라 결과가 다르다.

너무도 잘생긴 옹기 굴뚝. 나의 소장품 중 가장 으뜸이다. 한국인의 정신과 美가 물씬 느껴진다. 옹기 장인께 존경과 감사를 표한다. | Very handsome onggi chimney pipe, The best piece in my collection! See the spirit and beauty of Korean people. I extend my respect and gratitude to the onggi potter.

이러한 모든 조건은 바람이 불고 비가 내리며 가을에 단풍 드는 것과 같다. 오지그릇들의 불룩하고 미끈하고 붉은 듯 노르께한 갈색이 감도는 모습에서 느껴지는 변화는 산을 보는 듯하고, 단풍을 보는 것 같기도 하다.

옹기는 자연과 가장 친밀한 그릇이자 삶을 담아낸 그릇이며 자연과 모성을 품어낸 그릇이고 과학 그 이상의 그릇이다.

우리의 장류는 곰팡이, 세균, 효모 등의 대표적 미생물이 자연적으로 발생하여 어우러진 복합 발효 식품이다. 그리고 최상의 조건에서 산소에 노출된 형식으로 만들었기에 자연과 가장 친밀한 발효 식품이다. 또한 저장 방식이나 식성에 따라 새로운 가능성을 품고 있으며 미생물의 지표 물질이 생성되는 생리합성 식품이다.

옹기를 빚는 과정은 변수가 많아 일정한 공식이 없다. 그럼에도 숨 쉬는 옹기의 제작 과정에서 옹기의 소성은 가장 큰 요소로서, 그중에서도 가마 온도 맞추기가 아주 중요하다. 옹기의 소성은 피움 불, 중불, 큰불, 창불로 나뉘어 단계별로 진행된다. 마지막 단계인 1,210°C로 굽는 과정에서 점토질과 모래 알갱이

수탉 문양의 큰 항아리(옹기)
손가락 마디로 눌러 찍은 무늬띠. 활발한 필치로 뛰노는 수탉을 묘사했다.

Large Hangari Pot with Rooster Design
A patterned band pressed into the surface using finger knuckles. A running rooster is depicted with vigorous strokes.

가 고열에 의해 이완되면서 그릇 전체 표면에 미세한 숨구멍이 생기게 되고 숨 쉬는 옹기가 태어나는 것이다. 이렇게 만들어진 옹기는 웬만하면 깨지지 않는 강도를 지니고 있다. 바람의 피해를 막기 위해 흠이 있는 옹기로 세워서 '불막이' 혹은 '불매기'라 한다.

　가마에 최초로 불 지피는 단계인 피움 불 혹은 만불은 약한 불로 습기 제거를 위해 2~3일 정도 피움 불을 유지한다. 그 다음 단계인 중불로 옹기에 묻어있던 검댕을 열에 의해 연소시킨다. 이를 백금불 혹은 베낌불에서 제거되는 것으로 보고 옹기장이들은 옹기가 '옷 벗는다'라고 한다. 이는 옹기장이가 소성 단계를 파악하는 척도이다.

　세 번째 단계인 큰불은 1,100~1,200°C 정도에서 소성한다. 마지막 단계인 창불은 순간적인 고온으로 옹기를 익힌다. 창 구멍 통해 불의 상태와 옹기 표면의 윤기가 나는지 확인하며 불을 땐다. 붉다 못해 백색에 가까운 빛이 나면 그대로 둔다.
　가마 내부 윗부분을 '깃'혹은 '지새'라고 한다. 설익었으면 창솔을 가로질러 눕혀서 옹기 위에 걸쳐주는 데 이를 '깃 걸어 준다'라고 표현한다.

장독쟁이들에 의해 단순 처리되고 있는
장독 회화의 풍경들 우리 조상들의
소박한 美 의식을 나타내고 있다.
Nov. 30'20 심

옹기 꺼내기는 냉각 과정을 거친 뒤에 진행되며 전통 가마에서는 최소 이틀에서 닷새 이상 식혀야 한다.

옹기는 용도에 따라 종류도 가지각색이고 고을마다 명칭도 달랐다. 형태와 이름이 각자 자유분방한 특징을 지녔던 이유는 옛 선인들의 너그럽고 풍요한 마음가짐이 반영된 것이라 생각된다.

4

질그릇 예찬

"도점陶點에서 소줏고리를 굽는다."

목민관이 가져야 할 도리에 대해 서술한 책인 정약용의 『목민심서』에 따르면 소줏고리 기명을 '고오리(소줏고리의 속명)'로 표기하였고 '도점陶點'이라고 정확한 질그릇을 표현했다. 이렇듯 옹기는 민중과 함께 호흡하며 발달한 그릇이고 생활문화의 소중한 축임을 알 수 있다.

옹기는 우리 조형 문화의 한 가닥 맥을 잇는 문화재로서의 가치도 함께 지니고 있다. 흙을 다루고 매만지던 옹기 장인의 얼과 항아리에 내려앉은 세월의 때를 닦아내던 순박한 한국 여인네들의 생활 정서가 고스란히 담겨져 있다. 오지그릇의 생김새는 지극히 평범하면서 익살스럽고 모든 것을 포용하는 아량과 덕을 지니고 있는 것처럼 보인다. 가장 적합한 조화의 느낌을 주고, 자연(소나무, 산, 바람, 구름 등)과도 일체형이 된다.

소줏고리
발효 음식을 만드는 숨 쉬는 옹기는 생활 인테리어에까지 활용 가능하다. 그 친환경 기능에 감탄한다.

Soju-gori (traditional distillation appartus)
I marvel at the eco-friendly features of the respiring onggi used for fermenting food, even used for home decor.

술을 만들 때 사용하는 질그릇의 좋고 나쁨에 따라 술맛이 달라진다. 이는 술 만드는 과정을 한 가지만 보아도 알 수 있다. 술밥 담그는 데는 반드시 깨끗해야 한다. 샘물은 맛이 달고 차가워야 한다. 술밥을 찔 때는 불을 반드시 알맞게 (처음은 약하게 나중에는 세차게) 맞춰야 한다. 술밥을 담글 옹기의 선택과 완성까지 정성 다할 것을 기술하고 좋은 질그릇을 사용할 것 권고한다.

우리나라에 온 외국인이 옹기를 한 번 보고 나면 끌리지 않으려고 노력하는데도, 다시 보고 싶어 한다. 이것이 조선 질그릇의 매력이다. 우리 옹기는 음식을 담을 뿐 아니라 한국적 정신과 한국미가 담긴 옹기는 경쾌함, 근신함, 인내함 같은 은근한 덕에서 우러나는 미가 서려 있기 때문이다. 민족 정서가 표현된 질박한 아름다움과 너무 소박해 가식 없는 것이 옹기이며, 우리 문화이다. 자연과 함께 스스로 숨 쉬는 생명의 그릇이다. 우리 문화의 슬기를 담은 '옹기 엑스포'에서 전시된 무궁화 문양, 태극기 문양이 민족의 그릇임을 나타낸다.

임진왜란을 일명 도자기 전쟁이라고 부르는 이유는 당시 조선의 도자기를 약탈하고 조선의 도공陶工들을 붙잡아 갔기 때문이다. 조선인이면서 침략자의 땅으로 끌려가 일본인으로 살던 그들에게 가장 큰 비극은 내면을 혼란에 빠트렸던 정체성의

회령 솥단지 (함경도, 고성광)
Hoeryong Caldron (sotdanji), Hamgyong-do, Goseong-gwang

혼돈이었다. 그 비극성에 대한 통찰을 통해 우리 삶의 정체성의 문제도 돌아보게 만드는 까닭이다.

질그릇 하나에 평생을 바치면서 인생과 예술을 발견하는 도공들 모습이다.

'움직이는 물레(점토를 회전 시켜 질그릇을 빚는 기구)' 안에 움직이지 않는 한 점이 있는데 도공은 이것을 가리켜 심이라고 부른다. 이 움직이지 않는 심을 찾아가는 것이 도공의 일생이다. 그 심을 발견할 때 한 사람의 인간으로서 당당하게 살아갈 수 있으리라.

식생활에서 장이 차지하는 비중이 높았던 만큼 장을 담그는 옹기도 소중하며 또한 장독대에 대한 관심은 일종의 신앙으로까지 발전했다. 여기서도 우리 조상의 지혜를 볼 수 있다.

"과거 장 항아리는 민간 신앙의 대상, 잡귀가 범접하지 않도록 버선과 솔가지를 걸어두었다."

저장용 옹기는 지역에 따라 차이 있으나 일반적으로 큰 옹기를 형태적 측면에서 부항단지, 분粉 항아리, 양념 항아리 등으로 분류하였고 인분人糞 저장용 항아리와 물, 쌀, 장항아리 등으로 나눌 수 있다.

물 항아리 중에는 조선시대 다섯 집 기준으로 한 개씩 땅 속에 물을 채워 보관했다가 화재 발생 시 방화용으로 사용했던 대형 항아리도 있었다. 이렇게 쓰임새가 매우 다양하다.

옹기장이의 기술 숙련도는 큰 항아리를 몇 대에 걸쳐 물려받았느냐에 따라 가문의 내력을 살펴볼 수 있다. 짧은 시간 안에 장인의 키보다 큰 항아리가 빚어지는 모습을 본 외국인은 감탄하곤 한다.

일반 가정 장독대에 견주어 왕실의 것은 '염고'라 하고, 책임 상궁의 것을 '장고마마'라 한다.

버선본을 붙이고 금줄을 치는 어머니의 마음에는 가족들의 강녕과 행복을 기원하는 마음이 담겨있다.

5

옹기의 세계무형문화유산 등재 이유

1998년 4월 24일 MBC 특별 다큐멘터리에서는 국립중앙과학원에서 발표한 옹기의 통기성에 대한 연구 결과를 방송한 적이 있다. 1,200°C에서 잘 구워진 옹기를 전자 현미경으로 관찰한 결과 결정수結晶水가 빠져 나간 자리에 생긴 무수한 숨구멍을 통해 석영, 장석 그리고 운모로 구성된 옹기의 조직에서 석영 입자가 커지고 개수도 많아지면서 석영의 기공을 통해 통기성과 옹기의 강도를 제고시켰다는 것이 그 내용이다. 이와 같이 발효식품의 옹기는 '숨 쉬는 옹기'이라야 한다는 사실이 밝혀졌다.

옹기는 일상생활에서 가장 긴요하게 쓰여 온 그릇이다. 예부터 통기성이 다소 낮은 것은 물 저장용 옹기로, 통기성이 적당한 것은 발효식품용 옹기로, 통기성이 높은 것은 곡물 및 과실류의 저장용 옹기로 사용했다. 신석기 시대부터 우리 민족과 함께해 온 옹기는 한반도의 다양한 발효식품을 만드는 데에 그치지 않고 다용도로 사용했을 것이다. 옹기는 이렇듯 민족의 식문화에 부응하며 오늘에 이르게 되었을 민족의 그릇이며, 세계에서 유일한 그릇이다.

유네스코에 등재된 김장 문화도 발효 과학에 기초하고 있으며 민족의 건강에 핵심적 역할을 맡아 발전하는 옹기 문화가 그 토대를 마련하였기에 가능했으리라 생각한다.

나아가 숨 쉬는 옹기가 세계무형문화유산에 등재되어야할 이유는 다음과 같다.

첫째, 옹기장이들이 전통을 계승한 솜씨와 정열을 다 바쳐 성실히 옹기를 생산하는 데 있다.

둘째, 옹기의 소성 분위기가 산화-중성-환원 등으로 자동 조절되는 것은 우리나라 옹기 가마의 독특한 구조(조대불통 가마는 불통과 가마 칸이 90도로 꺾여 만들어져 있는 매우 특수한 구조로 세계 유일하다) 덕분이다.

셋째, 숨을 쉬는 음식인 발효식품을 담는 그릇으로서 숨 쉬는 옹기는 자정력自淨力으로 조절하는 데서 젖산균을 증가시켜 비타민C를 발생할 뿐만 아니라 정장整腸 작용까지 촉진시키는 데서 가지는 그 우월성이다.

우리나라 회유 옹기는 천년이 넘는 유구한 역사 과정에서 시종일관 '숨 쉬는 옹기'로서 자리를 지켜왔으며 이것은 실로 자랑스러운 일이다.

우리 음식의 80%는 장류와 각종 젓갈류인 발효식품이고 '감칠맛'을 내는 아미노산의 농축도 양적으로나 질적으로나 우리나라를 따라올 나라는 없다. 이것을 오래 저장할 수 있는 것은 회유 옹기인 숨 쉬는 옹기가 있었기 때문이다.

바로 이 점이 숨 쉬는 옹기일 뿐 아니라 발효식품을 만드는 옹기로서 세계적으로 독보적인 존재임을 증명하고 '숨 쉬는 옹기'가 세계무형문화유산으로 등재되어야할 이유다.

넷째, 옹기로 뭐든 만들 수 있고 그 쓰임새가 다양하다는 점 또한 장점이다. 옹기는 요즘 시대도 충분히 멋을 내면서 편리하게 사용할 수 있다. 그 예로 물두멍을 부엌 부뚜막에 놓고 아궁이에 불을 때면 더운물을 겨울에 사용할 수 있고, 물을 저장하면 자정력으로 식수로 쓸 수 있고, 허드렛물을 모아서 밭에 채소를 기를 수 있어 좋다. 이러한 옹기의 유용성은 20여 년의 무수한 시행착오로 끝에 '적정 온도'인 1,210°C에서 구워내어 웬만하면 깨지지 않는 강도를 지니고, 옹기는 열을 품는 특성 때문에 따뜻함이 오래 지속된다는 특징 덕분이다.

다섯째, 한국 세라믹 기술원에서 강도 및 흡수율 실험도 마쳐 자연과 함께 숨 쉬는 전통 옹기는 이로써 종합적이고 과학적인 근거를 마련했다. 옹기는 흙과 유약만으로 만들 수 있고, 깨져도 다시 자연으로 돌아가는 친환경적인 성격 때문에 플라스틱 쓰레기 문제의 해결책 중 하나가 될 수도 있다. 옹기의 가능성은 무궁무진하다.

정영목 교수가 소개한 거트루드 워너 소장 사진들 중 하나. 1920년대 조선의 '김장 풍경'.
(서울대학교 출판문화원 제공)

또한 한 민족의 장 문화와 함께했다는 사실과 과학적 근거로 연속되어 왔다는 점이 숨 쉬는 옹기의 발효 과학을 증명한다.

우리나라의 김장 문화는 2013년 12월 5일 유네스코 인류무형유산으로 등재되었다. 이로써 우리는 김치 종주국으로서의 입지와 정체성을 확립할 수 있게 되었으며, 더불어 발효 강국의 위상을 대내외적으로 알리고 인정받는 쾌거를 이루는 계기가 된 것이다.

한반도의 발효 문화는 그 원년의 뿌리가 깊고 사용되는 재료가 다양하다는 특징을 가지고 있다. 2500년 전에 쓰여진 중국 최초의 시가집 『시경』에 "외를 깎아서 저菹*를 담자"라는 문구를 통해 김치의 발효 문화를 알 수 있으며, 고려의 이규보(1168~1241년)의 『동국 이상국집』에서는 발효와 연계된 저장법과 절임법을 알리고 있다.

---
* 염채(鹽菜)를 뜻하는 것으로 문헌상으로는 김치의 시작을 알리는 시책인 셈이다.

십자가 무늬가 새겨진 장소레 (장독의 뚜껑)
Turned upside down, a jar lid can be used to hold water or other objects.

발효 식품의 토대가 된 옹기 문화를 알 수 있는 또 다른 서적으로는 조선의 실학자 서유구의 『임원경제지』**가 있다. 이 책에서 "옹기는 일상생활에서 가장 긴요하게 쓰이는 그릇으로 장을 담그거나 소금을 저장하며, 김치를 담그는 데 쓰인다"라고 하였다. 옛 서적에서 알 수 있듯이 옹기는 민족의 식문화에 부응하며 오늘에 이르게 되었다.

결국 김장 문화의 유네스코 등재를 통해 발효 과학의 기초가 되었고, 김치를 담아낸 숨 쉬는 옹기가 마땅히 세계무형문화유산에 등재되어야 하는 이유이다.

** 『임원경제지』: 조선 실학자 서유구가 쓴 조선 후기에 농업 정책과 자급자족의 경제론을 편 실학적 농촌경제 정책서. "옹기는 일상생활에서 가장 긴요하게 쓰이는 그릇. 장 담그거나 소금을 저장하며 김치를 담그거나 소금을 저장하며 김치를 담그는 데 쓰인다"라고 적혀있다.

6

북한 옹기

1) 회령 북청 옹기 또는 북청 물두멍

회령 도자기는 유선으로 완성하며
부드럽고 은은한 색조가 아름답다.

　북한 5도 옹기인 회령 도자기 옹기는 함경도 지방의 특산물로 형태에서 주는 정숙함을 겸비한 소박미는 독특하다. 회령 도자기는 순전한 민요(한국 지방 가마)나 오지라서 교류도 많지 않고 누구의 간섭이나 속박도 없이 도공이 마음먹은 대로 아주 자유롭게 그 지방의 여유를 꽃 피우며 만들어진 도자기라 생각한다. 무기교無奇巧, 일상의 용도 이외에는 하등의 목적도 없는 물건이기에 아름다움을 위해 인위적으로 가공해야 한다는 걱정 없이 빚은 것이다. 회령 도자기를 빚은 도공은 신과 통하는 자연인이라 해도 과언이 아니다.

　회령 옹기는 함경북도 회령 지방에서 만들어졌기에 붙여진 이름이다. 한반도의 유구한 역사와 함께해 온 회령 옹기는 한반도에서는 북방계 옹기를 대표하며 내화성이 강한 목질 점토를 태토胎土로 한다. 지역에 산재하는 흙과 재료를 사용하여 새로운 발견으로 이뤄낸 우리의 전통 생활 옹기이다.

　회령 옹기는 유색의 발색이 깊고 아름다운 것이 특징이며 인위적인 가공이나 금속 산화물을 사용하지 않고 모두 주변 자연에서 얻어진 나무와 풀로 유색을 만들어내는 고도의 기술로써 완성된다.

회령 10각 단지
꿀이나 차를 담아서 사용했던 것으로, 평각이 아닌 유선으로 완성되어 부드럽고 은은한 색조가 아름답다. (함경도, 정양섭)

Ten-sided Hoeryong Danji (Hamgyong-do, Jeong Yang-seop)
It was used to store honey or tea, and features a streamlined shape rather than a square shape, enhancing the beautiful soft, subtle color tones.

회령, 북청 옹기는 세간에 알려지지 않은
또 하나의 함경도 명품 옹기이다.

그 고장 사람들은 옹기를 이고 서울로 내려와 북촌과 사직동 일대에서 물장수를 하였다고 한다. 남한에 남아있는 회령, 북청 옹기는 이 과정을 통해 전해진 것이며, 이것이 전부이다. 북청 옹기의 또 다른 명칭은 북청 물두멍이라 한다.

현재 북한에서는 경성 부근에 위치한 함경북도 주을에서 중국과 러시아 관광객들을 겨냥한 관광 상품으로 회령 도기와 북청 도기가 생산되고 있는 것으로 알려져 있다.
회령 도기의 아름다움이 임진왜란을 전후한 시기에 일본으로 전해져 일본이 자랑하는 3대 도자기(라쿠야키, 하기야키, 가라쓰) 중 하나인 가라쓰 도자기의 발색 기술에 원천을 제공한 역사가 있다.

차호
차를 담아두고 사용하는 차통으로, 회령 도기의 유약에서 백자의 유색같이 하얀색으로 완성하는 작업은 고도의 기술이 요구되는 과정이다. (함경도, 정양섭)

2) 개성, 해주 옹기

고려 유신이었던 개성 사람들은 탁월한 상술로 사업을 확장했고 남북 교역의 중추적 역할을 했다. 조선 후기에는 송방이나 송도 상인들은 여느 귀족 못지않게 풍성하고 넉넉하였다. 조선의 귀족 문화이던 백자를 사용하기보다는 좋은 옹기를 별도 주문하여 사용했던 것으로 추측된다. 개성에서 만들어진 옹기 중에는 석간주 유약으로 소성된 것들을 많이 볼 수 있는데 수려한 목선의 주병, 신선로, 향로 등 아름답고 고급화된 옹기류를 볼 수 있다.

해주 항아리는 밝은 백토에 하늘빛 청색이 어우러져 최고의 아름다움으로 완성된 옹기이며, 이는 상류 계급의 상징으로 인식되기도 하였다.

14세기 아라비아 상인들을 통해 페르시아에서 수입된 코발트는 당시 황금보다 비싼 고가의 재료였다. 중국을 거쳐 조선으로 유입된 청화 안료는 최고급 도자기에만 사용되는 특권층의 전유물이었다. 그러나 19세기 들어서 서양 화학 결합 안료가 대량으로 유입되었고 대량 생산을 통해 대중화되면서 서양청유인 양청이라 불리기 시작했다. 이 안료로 관서 지방의 자연적 풍토와 특징을 담아 민화풍으로 그려내어 연질 백토에 청화 그림을 넣어 완성된 것이 해주 항아리이고 이 시기의 옹기들은 옹기를 성형, 소성하는 기법까지 오지그릇과 아주 유사하게 생산되었다.

회령 항아리

일본의 전문 공예지 『역목경위』에는 다음과 같은 글이 실려있다. "회령 도자기를 보았다. 정말로 경이적인 것이다. 유색 종류의 다양함이 예상 밖이었다. 특히 유약에서 느껴지는 깊은 호수 같은 맛과 형태에서 주는 정숙함을 겸비한 소박미는 점잖으면서 솔직하며 남조선 어디에서도 볼 수 없는 것이다. 회령 도자기는 한국의 지방 가마였다." (함경도, 최미경)

Hoeryong Hangari (Hamgyong–do, Choi Mi–kyung)

The following article is published in 『Yeongmokgyeongwi』, a Japanese magazine specializing in craft. "I saw the Hoeryong pottery. It's truly breathtaking. The variety of colors was unexpected. Especially with the rich glaze color resembling the deepest lake and the subtle presence combined with simple beauty, it is the embodiment of modesty and candor which cannot be found anywhere else in South Korea. Hoeryong pottery was a local kiln in Korea."

북한 지역 옹기인 회령옹기, 해주옹기, 북청옹기

북한 지역 옹기인 '회령 옹기'는 문화적 가치뿐 아니라 예술적 가치도 높다. 개성 중심으로 옹진, 연백 지방, 개성, 해주 옹기가 수준이 높았던 것으로 볼 수 있다. 피란 중에 챙겨온 한두 점의 옹기 유품으로 보건데 북부 지역을 대변할 수 있는 지형의 특징을 가지고 있으며 충분히 재조명할 연구대상이다. 북청 옹기는 세간에 알려지지 않은 또 하나의 함경도 명품 옹기이다.

해주 백 항아리

해주 백 항아리는 한수 이북 지방까지 확산되어 오지항아리의 영역을 점령하기도 하여 조선 도자기의 이단아처럼 불리기도 하였다. 백 항아리 장독대는 부유한 집안의 상징이었다. 특히 물고기, 모란꽃, 누각, 십장생 등으로 한껏 아름다움이 표현된 항아리는 실내의 쌀독, 꿀단지, 양념단지, 경옥고 단지 등으로 사용되었다. 김치와 장을 담은 것은 실외에 둔다.

고졸미故拙美는 옛 도공의 숨결과 몰아의 경지를 가늠하기에 충분하다. 현실은 부족한 자료와 무관심 등으로 옹기 문화의 진정성이 드러나지 못하는 것 또한 안타까운 현실이다.

바람은 우리 콩으로 메주 만들고 자연의 유익균이 착생된 것으로 통기성과 저장성이 좋은 '숨 쉬는 옹기'에 담아서 참으로 유익한 전통 장을 찾아내는 건강한 식탁을 완성했으면 한다.

북청 항아리
양각으로 돌출하여 새긴 용의 형상이 마치 살아있는 것처럼 표현되어 있고, 몸통은 양편의 손잡이로 활용되게 고안되었다. 항아리의 표면에 공작이 비상하는 문양을 음각으로 완성하여 조형미는 물론 예술적 가치가 높다. 함경도 북청 옹기 중에서 양각된 옹기로서 예술적 가치가 높다. (함경도, 마광현)

Bukcheong Hangari (Hamgyong-do, Ma gwang-hyeon)
The jar was formed to project the shape of a dragon in relief making it seem as if it were alive, and the dragon's body was designed to serve as handles on both sides. It shows a surface finish with an intaglio design featuring a flying peacock which is an indication of its high artistic value as well as formal beauty. Decorated with raised relief decoration, the onggi has high artistic value among the Bukcheong pottery in Hamgyong Province.

일제 강점기인 1937년 7월 일본 세균학계에서 '장유 속성균'의 발명이라는 명목하에 조선 가정의 경제적 부담을 줄일 수 있다는 논리를 앞세워 조선 총독부 특령으로 각 가정 장독대 철거령이 내려지기도 했다. 이렇게 전통 장류마저 농락 대상으로 취급되며 소중한 한반도 식문화가 단절될 심각한 위기에 처해 있었다. 또한 일제 강점기는 우리의 전통 기술을 말살했다. 황국균을 배양할 것을 고지함으로써 대량 생산 방식으로 우리의 장류인 곰팡이, 세균, 효모 등을 만드는 전통 기술을 말살했다.

이에 대한 대책으로 일제 강점기에 단절된 전통 가양주 역사를 교훈 삼아, 우리 전통 장류 식품의 원형 복구를 위해 영세 농장의 개발 및 교육 지원은 물론 전방위적인 연구를 기대해 본다.

나아가 우리 민족의 콩 발효식품이 세계적인 슬로우 푸드 Slow food로 거듭나기를 고대한다.

회령 주전자
일본의 미학자 야나기 무네요시는 "자연에 뿌리내리지 않는 물건은 세찬 기후와 싸울 수 없다. 그리하여 회령 도자기는 자연의 요구로 생긴 것이다. 두꺼운 유약을 입고 있는 회령 도자기는 자연과 합일한 아름다움의 전형이다."라고 말했다. - 오마이뉴스 기사 중에서 (함경도, 고성광)

Hoeryong Kettle (Hamgyong-do, Go seonggwang)
Japanese aesthetician Yanagi Muneyoshi said, "Objects that are not rooted in nature cannot fight against the harsh climate. Therefore, Hoeryong pottery was created in response to nature's demands. Showcasing its thick glaze, Hoeryong pottery is the epitome of beauty in harmony with nature." (From 'Oh My News' article)

감사의 말

우리만의 정서와 전통이 어우러져 있는 옹기가 전해주는 한국의 긴 역사와 그 안에서 전해지는 어떤 묵직한 무게감과 고유한 분위기는 그 어떤 것과도 대체할 수 없다고 생각한다.

새로운 시각으로 숨 쉬는 옹기에 접근해야겠다는 점과 태고 이래의 장구한 세월의 시간성, 민간에 널리 보급되는 광대한 공간성까지를 지니는, 그것을 기점 삼아 이 글을 쓰고자 했다.

우리의 숨 쉬는 옹기에는 흙의 기분을 마음껏 누릴 수 있는 자연이 함께하고 옛것에 대한 그리움, 생명력 등을 느낄 만한 매력이 있다. 옹기의 제작기법을 탐구하면서 손으로 작업하는 숨 쉬는 옹기로부터 친근감과 편안함, 옛 할머니의 향수의 감흥까지 가닿았다. 그동안 자연을 고집했던 이유로 말미암은 어떤 예우나 긴장에서 해방될 수 있어서 좋았다.

'숨 쉬는 옹기'는 우리 민족이 삼국시대 이전부터 사용해 왔고, 지금 시대도 충분히 멋을 내면서 편리하게 사용할 수 있는 예술성이 있다. 옹기는 1970년대까지만 해도 일반 가정에서 널리 쓰였지만, 점차 우리 주변에서 사라져가고 있어 안타까움이

크다. 하지만 그렇기에 더욱 옹기로 뭐든 만들 수 있고, 쓰임새가 다양하다는 점을 널리 알리고 싶다.

　지금은 장독대의 항아리 외의 대부분은 박물관 가서야 볼 수 있고, 또한 국보나 보물 같은 문화재로 지정된 적도 없고 우리 주변에 흔했던 민속품 하나에 불과했다. 또한 옹기를 가르치는 곳도, 교수도 없었기에 지역의 옛 가마터나 장인을 찾아다니며 도제식으로밖에는 알 수 없었다.
　옹기에는 미세 기공이 있어 전통주 만들 때 술맛이 좋다. 강도, 흡수율 실험도 다른 도자기에 비해 옹기의 가능성은 무궁무진하다. 흙으로 빚었기에 사용하다 깨져도 자연으로 돌아가 친환경적이며 그 형태는 소박하면서도 멋스러운 옹기의 매력을 끊임없이 발굴해 많은 사람이 다시 찾을 날을 꿈꾼다. 옹기 굽는 사람을 점놈이라 천시하던 시대는 옛이야기가 되어 요즘은 젊은 제자들이 자발적으로 공방에 찾아오고 있어 큰 힘이 되고 있고 희망을 꿈꾸고 있다.

　한국 옹기의 가장 큰 특징인 '숨구멍'은 중국 옹기에는 없다고 한다. 1996년 명장 황충길의 냉장고형 김치 항아리가 1998

년에 공예 명장에 선정됐다. 황충길의 "대를 이을 사람이 없어서 안타깝다"라는 말을 귀에 달고 자란 아들 황진영은 대학에서 '과학적'으로 옹기 공부했고, 도예를 전공한 사람과 결혼하였다. 지금 이 옹기장이 부부는 "아버지의 느낌과 손맛"을 과학적인 데이터로 바꾸는 작업을 하고 있다. 아버지의 살아왔던 세월과 경험의 눈어림과 아들의 과학적 분석이 거의 동일하다는 게 놀라울 따름이다.

"선대부터 아버지까지 축적해 놓은 경험치가 바로 과학이었다는 걸 객관화해서 더 쉽게 만들 방법을 찾는 것"이라고 말하며 황진영은 아버지의 경험에 존경을 표하며 사람의 손과 디자인이 융합하는 길을 걷고 싶다고 덧붙였다.
"어른들은 먹고살려고 시작했지만, 나는 일이 좋아서 한다. 내 아들에게 이 일을 잇게 하고 싶다. 할아버지가 만든 옹기를 바라보던 그 아이가 또 흙을 만지고 가마에 불을 지피게 될지…"

그가 걸어가는 길은 옹기의 미래를 개척하려는 젊은이들에게 큰 힘과 희망이 되고 있다. 정부는 그를 인간문화재로 지정하는 등의 제도적 뒷받침을 통해 미래의 인재를 양성해야 할 것이다.

그 훌륭함을 먼저 알아본 외국인들에게 '귀한 큰 항아리'로 팔려 가는 게 아쉽다. 옹기의 원주인인 우리가 그 훌륭함과 소중함을 이제라도 깨닫고 지키는 것이 애국하는 길이라고 생각한다.

우리 생활의 밑바닥에서 가장 큰 도움을 주었음에도 불구하고 그 존재 가치를 제대로 인정받지 못했던 '숨 쉬는 옹기'를 "한국적인 것이 가장 세계적이다"라는 자부심으로 민족 그릇이라는 긍지를 심고 세계 속의 독특한 우리 것으로 만들어 오래도록 보존하여야 한다. 이러한 강한 집념을 바탕으로 '숨 쉬는 옹기'와 벗하고자 한다.

이 책을 출간하기로 마음먹고 난 이후로 분단의 아픔으로 지금은 가 볼 수 없어 더욱 귀한 북한 지역 5도의 옹기를 비롯해 한반도의 다채로운 옹기를 접했다. 이때 옹기마다 묻어있는 기억과 그리움을 느낄 수 있었다. 그리고 이것이 우리 문화의 소중한 일면이자 과거로부터 연속되어 온 역사임을, 또한 다시는 복구할 수 없는 '우'를 반복하며 살아왔음을 깨달았다.

이 책이 많은 사람에게 왜 '숨 쉬는 옹기'가 세계무형문화재로 등재되어야만 하는지 이해하는 데 자그마한 도움이 됐으면 하는 바람이다.

지금 세계 음식 문화가 자연주의로 회귀하는 움직임이 일고 있다. 이것은 곧 우리의 숨 쉬는 옹기로 만든 발효식품인 김치에 대한 관심이 높아지고 있음을 뜻한다. 김치 문화의 유네스코 등재는 발효 과학의 기초가 되고 민족 건강의 핵심적 역할을 맡아온 옹기 문화가 그 토대를 마련해 주었기에 가능했다고 생각한다. 또한 한국의 김치가 세계의 5대 건강식품으로 꼽힌 이유로는 유산균과 각종 비타민이 풍부했기 때문이라고 한다.

한국이 발효식품 왕국으로 불리는 연유는 다양한 발효식품을 만들어 먹고 있을 뿐만 아니라 그 식품의 저장과 보존에서 뛰어난 기술력 즉, 숨 쉬는 '옹기' 덕분일 것이다.

> "이스라엘 족속아, 진흙이 토기장이의 손에 있음같이
> 너희가 내 손안에 있느니라. (예레미야 18:6)"
> Like clay in the hand of the potter, so are you in my hand, Israel.
> (Jeremiah 18:6)

구약 성경의 예레미야 18:6 속 토기장이의 비유이다. 모든 것은 하나님 손안에 있다는 말씀이고, 하나님 손에 들리는 순간 놀랍게 쓰임 받을 수 있다는 뜻이다.

우리나라 옹기의 우수함을 알려주신 송재선 선생님께, 실제로 도자기를 만드시며 옹기의 개념 정리를 분명히 해주시고 그 우수함을 외국에 알리시고 이 책을 쓰는 데 큰 힘이 되어 주신 이화여대 도예과 조정현 교수께, 옹기의 매력과 옹기의 여러 장

점을 제작해서 옹기의 매력을 발견하고 특히 옹기를 끊임없이 개발해 많은 사람이 다시 찾게 하고 젊은 제자들이 자발적으로 공방 찾아오게 하여 옹기 문화 유지에 '큰 힘' 되게 해주신 장성창 아트의 정희창 대표께 감사드린다. 아울러 북한의 옹기를 여러 점 소장하시고 그 예술성을 알게 해주신 고성광 옹기 문화원 소장님께도 감사드린다. 이북 5도민과 지사님들의 도움으로 연구 자료의 작은 초석을 마련할 수 있었다. 아낌없는 도움과 위로를 주신 함경 남북도, 평안 남북도, 황해도 도지사님들께도 감사를 전한다.

임진왜란 이후 단절되었던 이 기술이 1920년대 최면재 씨에 의해 다시 복원되어 그 맥을 이어왔고 남북분단으로 인한 단교로 현재는 일본에서 수학한 국내 작가들이 재현하여 작품 활동을 이어가고 있다. 그리고 수많은 시행착오로 부산에서 젊은 도예가 신한균 씨가 회령 옹기를 재현했음을 치하한다.

회령 옹기를 실제 사용했던 사람들의 기억과 증언을 통해 확인된 유물을 기꺼이 내어주고 격려해 주신 회령군 출신의 월남 1세대 어르신들과 회령 시가도, 회령 인근의 가마터를 표시해주고 옹기를 생산했던 삼합 인근 지역의 유적지까지 확인하게 도와주신 그 열과 성에 큰 감사를 표한다.

홍익대 도예유리과 졸업 후 젊고 왕성한 활동으로 수많은 전시 경력 및 수상 경력과 더불어 국내외에서 쌓은 경력으로 한국도자재단에 등록된 김연수 작가는 예술 활동의 일환으로 미국을 방문한 이력이 있는 예술가로, MICA Maryland Institute College of Art에 마련된 작업실과 국내외 여러 작품을 소장한 것 등으로 우리 것의 멋과 아름다움을 알리면서 우리 옹기의 희망을 불러일으키고 있다.

나의 글에 미진한 부분은 부족한 저의 책임일 것입니다.

참고 문헌이 도움 되시기 바랍니다.

함경도 회령 옹기 화분
Hoeryong Onggi Flower Pot, Hamgyong-do

시

숨 쉬는 옹기

김덕신

한번 눈길 주니 헤어날 길 없네
수더분한 여인네 같아서
그 진가를 외국인이 먼저 알고
다시 만들기도 귀한 큰 옹기 항아리들이
무관심 속에, 해외로 팔려 가는 안타까움…
천대받던 옹기장이가
땀과 정성으로 빚고
고온에 구우니 단단해져서
담그면 맛이 좋아지고
조심스럽게 다루면 반영구적이고
혹 깨어지면 흙으로 돌아가
친환경적이고 삶에 유익한
세계 유일의 숨 쉬는 옹기
전통적, 과학적, 소박미를…
예술적이기도 하며
우리네 여인들의 부지런함으로
세월의 때를 닦아내던

장독대는
순박한 우리네 여인들의 정보 교환 장소이며
먼 길 떠난 가족의 안녕을 빌던 곳
숨 쉬는 옹기는 박물관 전시에서나 만날까…
가장 전통적인 것이 세계적이라는 말처럼
다시 찾는 관심과 사랑으로
젊은이들이 배우고자 하는 열의와 희망이
감사할 따름이다.

Poem

Respiring Onggi

Kim Duk Shin

As soon as I had seen it, I was lost

a countenance of a good hearted woman

its true value first seen in the eyes of foreigners

rare to bring their splendor back, the large earthenware pots

amidst indifference, such sorrow of being sold abroad.

The derided onggi potter

kneads the clay with beads of sweat and sincerity

fired with the heat of life, it strengthens

submerged inside the pot a flavor that dances on the tongue created

handle with care, it gives a gift of semi-permanence

if it breaks, it returns to the dust of the earth

reversing the loss of nature, it lives in usefulness

the world's only respiring pottery

born out of tradition, based on science, articulated in simple beauty

artistically it dwells as well.

Work of our diligent women

wiping away the stains of time,

Jangdokdae

a meeting place for our humble women to exchange information

to pray for the loved ones gone on a long journey to dwell in safety.

Will we only encounter respiring onggi in museum exhibitions…

As the saying goes, the most traditional rules the world

with lost interest and love found again

young people full of fire to learn and a vision of hope

my heart swells with gratitude.

참고문헌

- 양호일 『한국의 옹기 문양』, 『공간』 Vol.141, 서울공간사. 1979년
- 『The Korean Onggi, Potter』 Smithsonian Institution Press, Washington. D.C. 1987년
- Ewha Photo Diary, 『한국의 옛 옹기』 조정현, 이화여대 출판부 1997년
- 『옹기와의 대화』 정병락. 옹기민속박물관 1997년
- 『제3의 전통, 옹기의 원류를 찾아서』 이화여대 박물관. 2000년
- 『우리나라 옹기』 송재선, 동문선, 2004년
- 『옹기를 만드는 사람들』 국립문화재 연구소, 민속원, 김인규·이한승 2009년
- 『자연의 그릇, 옹기』 고성광, 토담 2012년
- 〈옹기〉 국립민속박물관 소장품, 국립민속 박물관. 2013년
- 『조정현의 도자 탐색』 논문 모음, 이유경 엮음. 띠움, 2019년
- 『조정현의 도자 이야기』 글, 작품모음, 이유경 엮음. 띠움, 2019년
- 『조정현 자연의 그릇, 옹기』 한반도 옹기 찾아 떠나는 고성광의 문화여행, 경기 동창 회보지 (옹기 1~15), 고성광 (한국전통 옹기 문화원 소장) 2013년
- 「흙으로 빚는 오래된 옹기의 매력」 한겨레, 2023년12월30일 25면, 정희창 대표
- 「KINDS 종합지」 〈옹기 관련된 모음〉, 1996년
- 「옹기제조과정」 뿌리 깊은 나무
- 〈울산 세계옹기박람회전〉 사진 김덕신
- 〈기획특집/ 옹기 문화〉 구성 김미애, 사진 이강범, ≪행복이 가득한 집≫
- 〈덕수궁 함녕전에서 재현된 우리 장독 재연〉 사진 김덕신
- 정양모, 한국의 그릇. 옹기 〈오지와 질 그릇의 어제와 오늘〉 전에 부쳐, 『월간미술』. 1990년12월
- 우리 문화의 슬기를 담은 '옹기 엑스포' 세계 최초 문화 엑스포. 사진 김덕신
- 「장독 – 한국인의 맛과 멋의 뿌리」 조정권 시인
- 汶川巧 『조선도자기 名考』 조선 공예 간행회, 1931년
- 예용해 『옹기의 종류』 인간문화재 문화재 관리국
- 양호일 「옹기 문양의 이해」 『공간』 vol.141, 서울 공간사, 1979년

English translation

Bibliographic References

- Yang Ho-il, 『Korean Pottery Patterns』, 『Space』 Vol.141, Seoul Space, 1979
- 『The Korean Onggi, Potter』 Smithsonian Institution Press, Washington. D.C.,1987
- Ewha Photo Diary,『Korea's Old Pottery』 Jo Jeong-hyeon, Ewha Womans University Press, 1997
- 『Dialogue with Onggi』 Jeong Byeong-rak. Onggi Folk Museum, 1997
- 『In Search of the Origin of Pottery, the Third Tradition》 Ewha Womans University Museum, 2000
- 『Korean Onggi』 Song Jae-seon, Dong Mun-seon, 2004
- 『People Who Make Pottery』 National Research Institute of Cultural Heritage, Folklore Center, Kim In-gyu and Lee Han-seung, 2009
- 『Nature's Vessel, Onggi』 Go Seong-gwang, Todam, 2012
- 〈Onggi〉 Collection of the National Folk Museum, National Folk Museum, 2013
- 『Jo Jeong-hyeon's Ceramic Exploration』 Collection of papers, edited by Yu-kyung Lee. Tium, 2019
- 『Jo Jeong-hyeon's Ceramic Story』 Text, collection of works, edited by Yu-kyung Lee. Tium, 2019
- 「Cho Jeong-hyeon's Nature's Vessel, Onggi」 Ko Seong-gwang's cultural journey in search of pottery from the Korean Peninsula, Gyeonggi Alumni Bulletin (Onggi 1-15), Ko Seong-gwang (Korean Traditional Onggi Cultural Center), 2013
- 『The Charm of Old Pottery Made From Clay』 Jeong Hoi-chang, Hankyoreh, December 30, 2023, page 25
- 『KINDS Comprehensive Journal』 〈Collection Related to Pottery〉, 1996
- 『Pottery Manufacturing Process』 Deep-rooted Tree
- 〈Ulsan World Pottery Expo〉 Photo by Kim Duk Shin
- 〈Special Feature/Onggi Culture〉 Miae Kim, photos by Kangbeom Lee, 『House Full of Happiness』
- 〈Our Jangdok Relics Reproduced in Hamnyeongjeon Hall of Deoksugung Palace〉 Photo by Kim Duk Shin
- Yangmo Jeong, Korean bowls. Pottery 〈Yesterday and Today of Earthenware and Oji〉, 『Monthly Art』. December 1990
- 'Onggi Expo', the world's first cultural expo containing the wisdom of our culture. Photo by Kim Duk Shin
- 「Jangdok – The Root of Korean Taste and Stylish」 Poet Jo Jeong-kwon
- 『Joseon Ceramics 名考』 Joseon Crafts Publication Society, 1931
- Yonghae Ye 『Types of Pottery』 Living Cultural Heritage Cultural Heritage Management Bureau
- Yang Ho-il 「Understanding Pottery Patterns」 『Space』 vol.141, Seoul Space, 1979

English translation

Respiring Onggi
Object of Admiration

Written and illustrated by
Kim Duk Shin

Preface

In 1974 when I was working at the library of the Missouri State University, one day an American professor whom I met in an elevator suddenly asked, "Do you know how far ahead the Korean invention of movable metal type was compared to Johannes Gutenberg's work?" At the time I was not able to properly convey my feelings of pride that "Jikji Simche Yojeol" published with movable metal type at Heungdeoksa Temple in Cheongju, Chungcheongbuk-do Province in 1377 preceded the Gutenberg Bible by 78 years, along with the pride* of being descendants of our nation's history that developed the movable metal type printing technology. This encounter led me to become more interested in my own culture later on, and my cultural pursuit continued returning to Korea in 1977, when I started collecting onggi ware (an earthenware Korean folk pottery) which is what inspired me to write this book.

It is, I believe, not an overstatement to say that the history of humanity is the history of pottery, given that the Christian beliefs about the creation of humanity, in which God created man from clay, and the invention of pottery, in which humans used clay to shape by hand and fire it to create clay pots, are almost intertwined. My efforts aimed at preserving Korean pottery and earthenware served as the starting point for conducting my extensive research.

---

* "Jikji Simche Yojeol," the oldest book printed in Korea predates the printing of the Gutenberg Bible in Germany (1455) by 78 years. It is a precious cultural heritage of Korea, printed with movable metal type at Heungdeoksa Temple in Cheongju, Chungcheongbuk-do in 1377" which evokes a sense of pride.

Onggi ("jar-vessel") is the most basic form of a bowl. It is a vessel that has played a key role in our food culture as a basic resource for our people. Onggi ware is found throughout Korean households at every level of society, from the King's "jangdokdae" (a platform where the onggi jars are traditionally placed) in the royal palace to the rural farmer's kitchen.

The history of Korean pottery illuminates the production of onggi ware can be traced back to the Yeonjil (soft earthenware) pottery in the Neolithic period which evolved into hard earthenware, and high-fired ash-glazed earthenware in the late Unified Silla period. In this process, it laid the groundwork for learning the manufacturing techniques of green-glazed celadon in the early Goryeo dynasty, and from these roots developed the "pi-saek" celadon in mid-Goryeo period and Joseon white porcelain (baekja), forming the two main representations of Korean ceramics along with the long lineage of porcelain that has lasted to modern times. It can be said that onggi ware which forms an integral part of the Korean culture created a foundation for pottery vessels on the Korean peninsula.

The impetus behind this book is to convey to those of us who live today and pass along to our descendants who will live tomorrow the wisdom and sophisticated tastes of our ancestors, who cultivated beauty fused with sincerity and love in their daily lives through the use of onggi.

Introduction

Respiring Onggi

When we hear the word "onggi," the first thing that comes to mind is the large storage pots and jars placed on jangdokdae. The Korean people's use of earthenware, which is the predecessor of onggi can be seen in the depiction of the kitchen scenes or female figures standing at the well-site among the Goguryeo tomb murals in the Three Kingdoms period. We can learn about the history of onggi by looking at the paintings from the late Joseon Dynasty that feature the everyday lives of common people and the royal court paintings, including how onggi was produced in Joseon times, the appearance of onggi kiln sites, and the peddler merchants using "chige" (A-frame wooden carrier) to carry huge loads of onggi jars for sale on their backs.

As the world's only onggi culture that is unique to Korea, it makes us wonder if there are other places in the world where people have been using the same form of pottery from thousands of years ago as they have in Korea today. However, the changing form of housing from a house to an apartment has been accompanied by dietary changes which has resulted in the gradual fading away of onggi culture from our surroundings.

My relationship with onggi is deep and long-standing. When I am tired and exhausted, I set out on an antiquing adventure in search of old traditional Korean items which lifts my spirit and rejuvenates my energy. Not only do I get to explore with my eyes, but also hold the items in my hands so that I can immerse myself in the beauty and style of my Korean cultural heritage. By stirring up conversation and asking questions about the various types, names, usages, and the distinct regional characteristics of onggi, each adventure turns into an effective learning experience as well as an emotional one. One day I was gifted a chimney top design called "yeonga" from a store owner which piqued my curiosity about our cultural heritage. I have yet to find something similar to mine.

Wanting to know more about onggi I went to the museum libraries and archives, kept scrapbooks as I visited the video resource centers and used bookstores, and took photos when I travelled to the rural areas. As the rural population moved to urban areas, the broken onggi wares were left abandoned in the yard of empty farmhouses. In some cases, I would see the discarded broken pots laying around that were once used by our ancestors with great care. Many times I would get upset thinking how difficult it is to make them again.

Onggi were designed by our ancestors using an original, scientific, and hygienic method to knead the clay through several processes, and after the clay is dried slightly, it is covered with lye made from a mixture of "yakto" (locally mined clay) and ash stirred in with water. Then a decorative pattern is carved into the surface of the pottery with a finger or a piece of wood which not only enhances the aesthetic and the porosity, but also allows us to admire the wisdom of our ancestors who were able to give the pottery its own distinctive appearance. After being dried in the shade to the extent that the clay body does not get cracked or damaged, and then dried out in the sun to become a "raw bowl," it is dried out again in the sun, and transferred to a kiln to be fired at a high temperature of around 1,200°C for ten days. During this process, the sand particles included in the body of the clay dissipate by high heat, creating microscopic holes on the entire surface of the vessel resulting in an onggi that respires. When the onggi that has been fired in this manner is tapped, it gives a unique clear sound, and the onggi lid is as heavy and durable as cast iron.

Korean condiments such as ganjang (soy sauce), doenjang (soybean paste), gochujang (red chili paste), and jeotgal (salted seafood) are fermented and stored in the respiring vessels, which provide food throughout the year and fill our hearts with warmth, abundance, and generosity. In the summer sticky impurities seep out from the inside of jangdok (earthenware container for storing soy sauce), and our mothers and grandmothers wiped them twice a day in the morning and evening so that the porous walls would continue to breathe. Housewives subtly took pride in their jangdokdae holding shiny pots, a symbol of their diligence.

The respiring onggi possesses a distinct form of its own, with its own characteristics influenced by the climate and the natural environment of the region it comes from, as well as its diverse functions and the personality of the potter. One such example is in the late Joseon dynasty, when Catholic believers escaped religious persecution by hiding in the mountains who adopted onggi making as a way to sustain themselves, drawing pattern of the Christian cross or ichthus(fish symbol)* to express their faith.

Natural, non-toxic, and non-hazardous the respiring onggi made from soil can last for decades even thousands of years if used with care. The remarkable quality of onggi is when broken to be thrown away, it is quickly back to earth as natural soil because of its cutting edge components causing no harm to the environment which is a serious problem we face today. However, during the period of Japanese colonial rule, the onggi was fired at a low temperature to save fuel, and the glaze was mixed with a chemical substance called gwangmyeongdan (lead oxide) to make it glossy, but due to the lead content within the glaze, toxins entered the food and the air holes of the onggi were blocked which prevented the natural fermentation of food. In the process, most of the artisans who made traditional onggi struggled to survive and the proud tradition of the respiring pottery was on the verge

---

* The Greek letters for "Ichthus" are the initial letters of the Greek word for Jesus Christ, Son of God, Savior, and the Greek pronunciation is a Greek word for fish.

of extinction and replaced by containers made of stainless steel and plastic. It is worth remembering that what is most traditional is what is most global and it is my hope that we all take the lead in cherishing our respiring onggi and promoting its excellence to the rest of the world.

Sourced from earth the clay is fired in a kiln which involves numerous painstaking processes, and only when it is crafted with upmost loving care and attention of the maker at every stage, onggi finally presents itself to the world. Scientific and deeply rooted in our history, the respiring onggi represents the only cultural element of Korea which maintains the longest tradition with our people until today.

In May 1991, the Korean government designated onggijang (onggi pottery making) as an important intangible cultural property, and in 2013 the kimjang culture (making and sharing kimchi) was inscribed as the UNESCO Intangible Cultural Heritage of Humanity. However, born from the soil and the honest sweat of work, the respiring onggi has not yet been inscribed onto the UNESCO Intangible Cultural Heritage list.

When writing this book, my goal was twofold. First, to spread awareness of why the scientific respiring onggi with its long history and great cultural significance in Korea should be inscribed on the Intangible Cultural Heritage of Humanity. Second, I hope that many people will realize that the beauty and artistry of the respiring onggi which lies in its unique simplicity is disappearing from our surroundings due to changes in the current housing culture and food culture, and that it is unfortunate we are not aware of the value and beauty of our heritage.

The respiring onggi belongs not only to us, but it is a common asset and cultural heritage shared by all humanity. Traditional onggi remains by our side embracing us with its generosity and warmth, and the beauty of empty space concealing the presence of what dwells within. It awakens our mind to the beauty and precious meaning of the unconscious.

Firing onggi ware is considered the most difficult and important process. It takes maximum effort to calibrate the temperature in the kiln. Most clays can sustain the firing temperature at 1,210°C. Using firewood as fuel for the kiln, onggi is fired for ten days, and the fermented food stored in onggi created by the true onggi masters are tasty and recognized for its health benefits.

Jang* is made with devotion

Soy sauce and soy bean paste made from high quality soybeans are free from artificial colors, flavors, and preservatives. The philosophy behind the Korean jang is centered upon the Five Virtues which serve as a connection between the mind, sincerity and the jang. The virtue of single-mindedness keeps its flavor even as it mixes with others, the virtue of perseverance stores the food long-term without spoiling, the virtue of mercy removes the fishy and greasy odor, the virtue of benevolence tones down the spicy element, and the virtue of reconciliation pairs well with any food.

In order to make good jang, the soybeans should not be overripe under the late autumn sun. The cooked beans are ground with a mortar until about 70% of the soybeans are crushed and kneaded to make meju (fermented soybean blocks). Once hardened, they are tied with rice straw and hung to dry through the winter. During this fermentation process, microorganisms flourish and sporulate which women in the olden days called it the blooming of Meju flowers. When the thaw comes, the first last day of the first lunar month in the calendar is regarded a "gil-il" (auspicious day), an ideal day for making traditional sauces.

The meju blocks are stacked inside a jar well sterilized with a straw fire and brine is poured until it fills up to the 7th

* salted and fermented paste or sauce

ridge of the jar. To prevent the meju from floating on top of the brine, bamboo sticks were inserted to act as a weight.

Red chili peppers, charcoal, and jujube are added on top of the brine which help to prevent the jang from changing flavor. The red chili peppers serve to add spiciness, the charcoals for their antibacterial properties and removal of impurities, and jujubes flavor the sauce with sweet notes at the same time strengthening the color red to ward off evil spirits. Janggeum straw rope (twisted in a left-hand unlike ordinary rope) intertwined with pieces of charcoal, peppers, pine needles, and changhojie (window paper) was loosely tied around the pot, and a paper beoseon-shaped (traditional Korean sock) pattern is pasted upside down on the body of the jar for protecting against insect invasion.

The basic ingredients for making jang sauces are water, salt, and beans, but a mother's tender loving care begins the next day. In the morning when the sunlight is warm, the lid of the jar containing the jang is removed to evaporate the brine, and put back on before the sun goes down. If white mold forms on the surface of the brine in the humid summer, it should be skimmed off, and during the fermentation the salty flowers on the outside of vessel should be cleaned regularly. Such care is said to be a crucial part of attaining great-tasting jang sauce. The "Respiring Onggi" accompanies this whole process.

An indispensable part of Korean identity, the "Respiring Onggi" is the epitome of natural beauty. The timeless beauty that exudes from onggi is the accumulation of time and care spent giving birth to the "Respiring Onggi," requiring the skilled hand of a master craftsperson using traditional techniques.

It is a mysterious earthenware with a porous structure that allows the vessel to breathe maintaining optimal conditions. Without the birth of onggi culture in Korea, the feat of the registration of kimchi, doenjang, and gochujang at the CODEX* would not have been possible.

---

* Joint FAO/WHO Codex Alimentarius Commission: An international food standards and guidelines setting body established as a subsidiary to the WHO

Chapter 1

Concept of Onggi

Onggi has been an important topic of interest among scholars not only in Korea, but it has also attracted significant attention from researchers around the world. In 1987 Robert Sayers, an American scholar whose research focused on onggi ware published a book "The Korean Onggi Potter"[*] using anthropological research methods rather than examining the history and definition of onggi or conducting a scientific investigation. Based on his observations of the onggi culture in the 1970s while he explored the country, Sayers's research presented the investigation, analysis, and summary of the field survey data.

This is nothing more than an intensive survey focusing on a specific period of onggi production which boasts a long rich history that has existed since ancient times. Although it can be pointed out that Sayers takes an anthropological approach to the study of onggi, yet this method filtered through the lens of cultural bias could lead to a similar situation in which the Japanese favoritism towards Goryeo celadon or Joseon white porcelain resulted in their status as antique objects.

---

[*] See 『The Korean Onggi Potter』 published by Smithsonian Institution Press in 1987.

When the achievement of onggi has not been sufficiently discussed and historical distortion takes place, there is a possibility it could undermine our understanding of onggi, as we have observed in our misconception of the history of Korean ceramics. This tendency also spread to the government offices and royal courts, and the term onggi was used interchangeably with pottery willingly.

Since onggi encompasses earthenware and earthenware has been made since time immemorial, onggi may be considered to be the very framework itself that forms the basis of Korea's ceramic history.

It is known that it was only recently that glaze was intentionally applied to earthenware. Onggi comprises the majority of earthenware and it may be said the number of "ot" ware by comparison was extremely limited. Our unique onggi is used as a comprehensive term that collectively refers to earthenware and "oji" earthenware, and is also used in a narrow definition to refer to large "dok" pots.

"Jil" onggi is earthenware that is fired without being unglazed, and "ot" onggi which is glazed. These "ot" onggi were initially called "oji" onggi and as they became common, the term onggi became popular and came to be known as the basis of glazed pottery. The pottery makers classify the pottery defined by the firing process into "jil dok," "phu-rae dok," "ban oji," and "oji."

When jil onggi is fired, the clay body shows a black-grey color due to the soot from the burning wood which provides a waterproof function to the vessel.

Pu-rae onggi involves a similar firing process as the jil onggi, but when the firing reaches a certain high temperature in the kiln, salt is sprinkled to the vessel. The potters refer to it as "salting," and depending on how much or less salt is added, it influences the glossy film on the surface.

The presence of pu-rae onggi indicates the making process was distinguished from the days of firing jil onggi without adding the salt.

The firing process of ban onggi uses the salting technique, but similar to the making of pu-rae onggi, the fire is not fed with soot and the vessel shows the natural colors from the reaction with the salt in the clay body. When the whole process is completed the glossy sheen on the surface gives the same effect of an oji onggi. However it is different from glazed earthenware.

Oji (ot onggi) is the type of onggi that is glazed and when the glaze melts it produces a glossy surface. Ot onggi was called oji onggi, and as it became common, the term onggi became popular and came to be known as the basis of glazed earthenware that is further supplemented by Seokganju mineral glaze.

The concept of onggi we are familiar with has evolved through this transition into what it is today. The stage before the ot onggi becomes a completed object is called a "ban oji" pot, which is different from pu-rae pot and involves a different creating process than the one used for oji onggi.

Previously we have summarized the differences in terms of composition and firing technique, but the important fact is that there is a significant difference in content that clearly distinguishes the oji onggi made only for onggi.

The unique characteristics of onggi are influenced by the region in which they are made, so the pots can be used to study the distinctive regional characteristics. Since each period has its own distinct characteristics of earthenware that provide a historical awareness to understanding the cultural practices and beliefs, onggi should be given due importance as a national cultural heritage.

The problem is the measures aimed at preserving onggi can only be achieved if there is awareness and considerations at the national level. The fact that such large quantities of onggi are being exported overseas indicates the value of onggi is internationally recognized, therefore, it can be developed and sold as a local product which provides a way of safeguarding traditional heritage and promoting the new to the world. The endeavor deserves to be greatly encouraged by the state government and it is hoped the onggi exhibition held at Deoksu Palace serves as a momentum to establish support measures and promote the importance of onggi.

Chapter 2

Lines and Patterns of Onggi

The Curved lines that define the symmetrical structure of the pot is shaped by the rotation of the potter's wheel, and the humble appearance of Korean onggi without a refined aesthetic, has a sense of simplicity and friendliness, offering a meditative space in which to contemplate its naturally flowing curvaceous beauty. The gently curving sides harmonize well with the decorated patterns enhancing the formative beauty of onggi. The beauty of lines created from the rhythm through the movement of the body and the potter's hand trajectory, and the onggi's patterns made of the repetition of wavy curved lines are asymmetrical, but it can be seen that the curved lines of the wave patterns that shrink or expand originated in the circle. to large "dok" pots.

The Interpretation of the Mandala

The elevated part of the radial patterns featured on the Korean onggi has an identical appearance to Carl Gustav Jung's* archetypal image of the mandala which symbolizes "a new world as a mountain rising from the collective unconscious." The sun as a ceremonial symbol represents the summit of the mountain. In other words, it can be seen the laws of nature and the flow of human imagination are formed and differentiated in the same subject-object relationship. This is simply because the utopian life of a potter represented in the onggi patterns such as weeds and grains, leaving the darkness of reality and expressing the act of libido through the primitive energy of molding clay, characterized by the traces and symbols which were manifested in the Korean peninsula around 1900 are considered to be the essence of onggi patterns.

On the Interpretation of Taegeuk

The most primitive of all symbols of power is the shape of Taegeuk. According to Carl Gustav Jung, the most well-defined concept of the creation of universe is the Eastern philosophy of Tao. It is certain that the onggi patterns will be remembered as the symbol of Taegeuk. The pattern on the "Gateway to Landscape" onggi discovered in Ganghwa Island which is believed to have been painted by an onggi master has a decisive formal value. This is regarded as the essence of onggi patterns. Before 1900 A.D. the human core desire to live well stemming from the unconscious world of the Koreans is made apparent through the space of onggi and jangdok. In the interpretation of Taegeuk, the most primitive of all symbols of power is the Taegeuk pattern, and according

---

* Carl Gustav Jung (1875–1961): A Swiss psychiatrist and pioneer of analytical psychology. He also developed psychological theories about mandalas and applied them to the field of therapy.

to Carl Gustav Jung, the Eastern Tao principle rests on a belief in the power to attract yin and yang and maintains the pattern of time. The combination of + and − where the law of nature exists, and furthermore, the harmony of yin and yang forms the basis of the general theory of organization from microcosms to microparticles. It is certain that the patterns will be remembered as the symbol of Taegeuk for a long time.

In aesthetic terms, the lines of hangari (large lidded onggi) in the southern provinces flow in wider curves than the jars in the central provinces.

In addition, the hangari shows morphological variations according to the regional climate. Food storage conditions are affected by sunlight exposure and the radiant heat stored in the ground, and the hangari's shape can also be seen as a reflection of wisdom coming from our ancestors' experience.

The variation in patterns by province can also be observed. The hangari from Seoul is characterized with its abundance of figurative patterns such as orchids and butterflies, while the one from Jeolla-do displays a wealth of motifs including wave patterns, bamboo and plant leaves. Due to the characteristics of the onggi kilns, the various vessel types produced by the different potters could be distinguished who began to engrave their own sign into the pottery surfaces resulting in the development of onggi pattern designs. In addition, the onggi made specially to order for a person of importance or to be used in a particular context was engraved with a specific motif that met the customer's needs.

Due to the persecution of the Catholic Church, the cross or the fish symbol of Jesus Christ used as a sign of faith among the believers, are often engraved on the inner wall or bottom edge of the onggi shoulder, and on the interior of the lid in an abstract form.

On the interior of the lid, we can find motifs in the form of the Chinese character of 井 ("water well") or the shape of a tree branch by two lines that intersect each other with a parallel line drawn from left to right and then a perpendicular line from top to bottom which form the Chinese character of 十 ("ten").

Most of the engraved designs on the outer walls of the hangari are simply patterns with the glaze removed, but the motifs such as the fish, pomegranate, and the grape are also found engraved in the form of negative-positive embossing or more rarely with openwork design.

Chapter 3

Air Holes of Traditional Onggi, the "Respiring Vessel"

The "Respiring Onggi" is not only used to make kimchi and various fermented foods unique to Korea, but also for storing these foods for long periods of time. Depending on the intensity of sunlight exposure which varies by region, the technological and utilitarian features of Korean pottery have cultivated to a high level and captured the hearts of the global pottery world. The shape of onggi has distinctive regional characteristics depending on the sunlight exposure and its usage. In addition, the firing process and the local climate and customs of each region, together with the sunlight exposure, all account for the onggi shape.

Due to the traditional food culture of the Korean people which requires long-term storage of fermented food, onggi in the Joseon society was destined to become an indispensable part of daily life as a storage container. It is part of the history on the Korean peninsula marked by the ingenuity in developing tools essential for daily life.

The origin of onggi, the high quality unglazed earthenware that has developed since prehistoric times, begins with the technique of shaping with clay, covered with lye and firing at a high temperature. The inheritance of traditional pottery making techniques and glazing techniques has formed the onggi into the most unique creative earthenware.

Onggi boasts an extremely modern shape. Despite these formal aesthetic qualities, color depth and diversity, onggi has been regarded only as a folk material representing the Korean traditions of everyday life.

Onggi has a distinctive range of unique color tones due to the harmonious use of fire. The brown earthenware is imbued with emotion deep-rooted in the hearts of the Korean people and represents one of the traditional Korean pottery. Onggi has been an integral part of the Korean culture for a long time and embodies the soul of our people, because it relates to a comfortable pace of life and flourishes with love and care for providing food for the family.

Science has proven that onggi has purification capabilities based on studies that demonstrate unboiled water stored in a respiring water jar is adequate for drinking.

The well-dried rice straw bundles (narak) used to skim the onggi produces the fermentative growth of Bacillus subtilis, which are microorganisms necessary in the fermentation process of Korean traditional "jang" sauces. The production of traditional fermented soy sauces is a scientific activity without greed. The main component of the traditional sauces is alkaline salt which has the ability to absorb and neutralize bacteria.

It is a scientifically proven fact that our ancestors knew how to connect the science of fermentation using the unique material properties of "dok" (onggi) with the Korean jang culture through the yin energy of clouds and rain, and the yang energy of the sun and clear sky.

Red chili pepper is an important spice in the fermented sauce. Due to the antibacterial and antiseptic effects of capsaicin contained in red pepper, the knowledge of using it for keeping the jang unspoiled during the fermentation process was developed through scientific reasoning. The wisdom of our ancestors can also be seen in the white "beoseon" (a traditional sock) pattern pasted on the body of the jar.

According to a study published in 2012 by Swedish scientists, the color pests hate the most is white. Our ancestors repelled insects by attaching a beoseon pattern to the jangdok jar. In this way the advances of modern science are uncovering the secrets behind onggi's traditional technology.

Sometimes a straw rope twined with pine needles is tied around the jar which serves as its protective guard against various germs. This is because as modern science has shown us, the needles on the pine trees secrete a substance called phytoncide which has antibacterial properties.

Various conditions must be met in a harmonious manner for the completion of onggi. The results vary depending on the onggi master's creative energy level on the day of making the jar, when and where the clay or "yakto" (locally mined clay) was dug up, which month of the year the onggi was fired, and the condition of the wind.

All these conditions are like the variation of elements in nature such as the blowing wind, the falling rain, and the changing autumn leaves. From the rounded bulge, the glossy surface, and the varying levels of the reddish and yellowish-brown color exhibited by the oji onggi ware, it feels like we are looking at the various hues of the mountain or the autumn foliage.

Onggi has the most intimate relationship with nature, a vessel of life embodying the abundance of nature like a mother's embrace, and a scientific wonder.

The traditional soybean-based sauce known as "jang" involves a complex fermentation process in which the representative microorganisms such as molds, bacteria, and yeasts are naturally formed. Because it is made under the best conditions that offer the permeation of oxygen, it is fermented food closest to nature. In addition, it offers new possibilities depending on storage method or diet, and is a biosynthetic food that produces microbial indicator organisms.

Since there are many variables in the onggi manufacturing process, there is no standard formula for onggi pottery. Nonetheless, the firing process is the most important factor in the production of the respiring onggi. and very critical among them is calibrating the correct temperature in the kiln. The firing process is classified into "water smoking fire," "middle fire," "large fire," and "window fire" and proceeds in stages. The final stage involves the process of firing at 1,210°C in which the sand particles in the clay body become passages and micropores are formed on the onggi's entire surface resulting in its breathable porous body. Onggi made in the way is known for its high impact strength. To protect from wind damage, onggi with flaws are erected which are called "bulmaki" or "bulmaegi" (windproofing).

The "water smoking fire" or the "beginning fire" which is the initial stage of kiln firing, is a weak fire maintained for 2-3 days to remove the moisture from the clay. In the next stage the "middle fire" burns the black soot covering the onggi with heat. Seeing this as the "platinum fire" or "baekkim fire" removing the blackness, the potters say that the pottery "takes off its clothes." This is the criterion by which the potter identifies the firing stages.

The third stage, the "large fire" corresponds to a temperature around 1,100-1,200°C. The final stage involves the "window fire" in which onggi is fired at a high temperature. The fire is built while checking the condition of the fire and the glossy surface of the pottery through the window opening of the kiln. When the red flame turns to white, the fire is maintained at a uniform temperature.

Inside of the kiln the upper part is called "git" or "jisae." When the onggi is half baked, the pine needles are hung horizontally above the jar, which is called "hanging the feather."

The onggi jars are unloaded after they are cooled off, and in a traditional kiln they must be left to cool for at least two to five days.

Just as the onggi is distinguished into various types depending on its usage, so too is the onggi name depending on the region.

Each shape and name of onggi characterized by its freewheeling spirited style is thought to reflect the mindset of the generosity and abundance of our ancestors.

Chapter 4
Admiration of Jil Onggi

Sojutgori is fired at the Dojeom(陶點)

In the 『Mongminsimseo』 (Admonitions on Governing the People), a book written by Jeong Yak-young in which he discussed the duties administrators were bound to perform, the name "sojutgori" (traditional earthenware for distilling brewed liquor to produce soju) was written as "goori" (the generic name of the sojutgori) and a perfect earthenware was called "dojeom"(陶點). As such, we can be see that the development of onggi, a living respiring earthenware was shaped together with the people which has been a valuable axis in Korean culture's everyday life.

Onggi also has value as a cultural property that connects a strand of the formalism in Korean arts. It is filled with the spirit of the onggi master handling and touching the clay soil, and the everyday life and sentiments of the unpretentious Korean women who diligently wipe the built-up dirt off the jars. Onggi appears extremely ordinary and humorous, and seems to be characterized with the virtue of generosity that embraces everything. It creates the most appropriate sense of harmony and becomes one with nature merging into the pine trees, mountains, wind, and the clouds.

The taste of "sul" (Korean alcohol) varies depending on the quality of the earthenware used to make it. This can be observed just by looking at the liquor production process. The bowl used for soaking the rice in water must be clean. Spring water must be sweet and cold. It is important to set the right level of fire (first with weak fire, then strong) when steaming the rice. The overall fermentation success requires the right onggi to soak the rice and attentive care, and it is recommended to use a good quality earthenware.

Even though foreigners who come to Korea try not to be drawn to the charm of onggi once they see it, they want to see it again. This is the appeal of Joseon earthenware. The reason is onggi not only stores food, but it is also imbued with the Korean spirit and its subtle beauty of virtues such as cheerfulness, prudence, and patience. Onggi has a simple humble beauty without pretense which represents the expressive body of Korean cultural identity. It is a vessel of life that respires on its own with nature. Onggi with the Mugunghwa (Rose of Sharon) and Taegeukgi patterns exhibited at the Onggi Expo which encompass the Korean culture full of wisdom represent the vessel of the nation. The absolute tragedy of the Imjin Invasion of 1592, the so-called pottery war, is the captured Koreans who were taken to Japan and forced to live as Japanese during the Imjin War suffered from confusion of identity and mind. It is through the deep insight into the tragic history that makes us reflect on the issues of identity in our lives.

The photograph*(page 55)* shows the potters who have explored many aspects of life and art through their lifelong dedication to making earthenware vessel.

As the wheel (a device that rotates a lump of clay to make earthenware) spins, the potters call a point of mass with no motion a "sim" (core). Searching for this immovable core is the life's journey of a potter. When one finds that "sim," one moves through one's life with a strong sense of self as a human being.

Since the "jang" fermented sauces or pastes make up a large proportion of the dietary life in Korea, onggi used for fermenting the sauces were considered precious and interest in jangdokdae developed into a kind of worship. Here we also see the wisdom of our ancestors.

In the past jang jars were objects of folk belief tradition, so to ward off evil spirits socks and pine branches were hung from them

Onggi used as storage containers show considerable regional variations, but in general large onggi ware is classified in terms of shape such as "buhang danji," "bun hangari," and hangari for spices, and it can be divided into "inbun hangari" (portable urinal), and storage jars for water, rice and jang sauces.

Among the water jars, there were also large jars filled with water buried underground for each of the five houses during the Joseon Dynasty and used for fire prevention measures in case of fire. As you can see onggi has a wide range of uses.

The level of a potter's technical proficiency can be detected according to how many generations the large hangari has been passed down within families. Foreigners often admire the way a pot taller than the height of a maker is formed in a short period of time.

Compared to the jangdokdae for ordinary households, the similar terraces of royal palaces are called "yeomgo," and the court lady's one is called "janggo mama."

Chapter 5

Reasons to Register Onggi as a World Intangible Cultural Heritage

On April 24, 1998, a special documentary aired on MBC TV that presented the research findings on the permeability of onggi conducted by the National Academy of Sciences of Korea. Using an electron microscope to examine the onggi fired at 1,200°C, the results of study show the crystal water contained in the wall of the onggi is released making the onggi porous and the number of sand particles in the onggi's clay body composed of quartz, feldspar, and mica increased through the countless micro-pores, and owing to its pore characteristics the air permeability and strength of onggi improved. Consequently, it was confirmed the respiring onggi should be used to ferment food.

Onggi is a vessel that has been the most essential item in Korean daily life. Since ancient times, onggi with low permeability have been used for water storage, moderate permeability for fermented food, and high permeability for storage of grains and fruits. Since the Neolithic Age onggi has been an integral part of the Korean life which must have been used for various purposes, not just for fermentation of a variety of food on the Korean Peninsula. Onggi has enriched Korean culinary culture in this manner and has become today a national vessel of Korea, the only one of its kind in the world.

Kimjang, the tradition of making and sharing of kimchi, which is also based on the science of fermentation was inscribed on UNESCO Intangible Cultural Heritage of Humanity list, and in my opinion this was possible because the onggi culture, which has evolved to play a key role in maintaining the health of the nation laid the foundation for the global recognition of kimchi.

Furthermore, the reasons why respiring onggi should be inscribed on UNESCO's intangible cultural heritage list are as follows:

First, the potters have devoted all their passion and inherited the traditional skills to faithfully cultivate the onggi practice.

Second, because of the unique structure of Korean pottery kilns the oxidation, neutralization, and reduction atmospheres are automatically adjusted when firing. Jodaeppeol bultong kiln has a special elongated structure in which the firing chamber and the combustion chamber are bent at a right angle, the only one of its kind in the world.

Third, the superiority of respiring onggi as a storage container for fermented food which is a living food, comes not only from the self-controlled permeability to produce vitamin C by promoting the growth of lactic acid bacteria, but also from the ability to help stimulate the bowel movements.

Over the course of more than a thousand years, Korea's onggi with wood ash glaze has consistently maintained its status as "respiring onggi," and this is indeed something to be proud of.

80% of Korean cuisine consists of fermented food made from jang pastes and various kinds of "jeotgal" (fermented fish), and in terms of quantity and quality no country's cuisine comes close to Korean fermented food concerning a high concentration of amino acids which give them their umami flavor. The fermented food can be stored for a long period thanks to the respiring onggi with ash glaze. This is the reason respiring onggi should be inscribed on the Intangible Cultural Heritage list since it proves onggi is not only a respiring vessel, but also a vessel that is unique in the world with its distinctive function in making fermented foods.

Fourth, onggi offers the advantage that it can be used for making many things and for diverse purposes. Today onggi continues to have both practical and aesthetic appeal. For example, if the onggi water jar is placed on the buttumak (traditional Korean kitchen fireplace) and the agungi (furnace) is lighted, it provides hot water in the winter, and onggi could be used for storing drinking water due to its purification capabilities, and for collecting water to be used in vegetable fields. As a result of 20 years of trial and error and countless failures, these functionalities developed by firing the onggi at the optimal temperature of 1,210°C in order to survive everyday use without breakage, and to acquire its ability to absorb and retain heat for an extended period of time.

Fifth, the Korea Institute of Ceramic Engineering and Technology investigated onggi's strength and absorption rate, thereby providing a comprehensive and scientific evidence for traditional onggi's capability to respire with the air of nature. Made of only clay and natural glaze, onggi can be one of the solutions to the planet's plastic waste problem due to its eco-friendly nature and when it is broken it can return to nature again. The possibilities of onggi are limitless.

In addition, the fact that onggi has been an integral part of the Korea's jang culture and that it has continued to develop the scientific basis of its permeability shows the science behind fermentation with the respiring onggi has been scientifically validated.

Korea's kimchi-making culture was inscribed on UNESCO Intangible Cultural Heritage of Humanity list on December 5, 2013. This enabled us to reaffirm our position and identity as the country of origin of kimchi, and also served as an opportunity to achieve the great feat of promoting and being recognized as the powerhouse in fermentation across the country and internationally.

The fermentation has deep-rooted traditions on the Korean peninsula stemming from the beginning of Korean civilization which is characterized by a diversity of food ingredients. In the 『The Book of Odes,』 the first collection of Chinese poetry written 2500 years ago, the phrase "cucumbers growing on the farm are shredded to make jeo (菹)*" indicates the use of kimchi fermentation, and in 『Dongguk Isangguk』 a collection of writings by Yi Gyu-bo (1168-1241) from the Goryeo Dynasty the methods of food preservation related to fermentation and pickling are mentioned.

Another literature that provides insight into the onggi culture which became the foundation of fermented food is 『Imwon Gyeongjeji』** (Sixteen Discourses on Rural Life and Economy) by Seo Yu-gu, a Silhak scholar in the Joseon Dynasty. He mentioned "Onggi is the most essential vessel in daily life, used for making sauce, storing salt, and fermenting kimchi." From the classical literature works, we can see the onggi as we know today has evolved by embodying the soul of the Korean food culture.

At last, as a UNESCO's intangible heritage, kimchi-making culture became a symbol of fermentation science, and this is the reason why onggi that respires used for fermenting and preserving kimchi should be inscribed on UNESCO Intangible Cultural Heritage of Humanity list.

---

* It refers to a vegetable pickle and it is the earliest recorded account of kimchi found in literature.
** In the book 『Imwon Gyeongjeji』, Joseon dynasty scholar Seo Yu-gu explained, "Onggi is the most essential vessel in daily life. It is used for making sauce, storing salt, making kimchi, storing salt, and making kimchi."

Chapter 6

North Korean Onggi

As discussed above, we examined the excellence, scientific principles, and traditions of onggi. Now we will look at the onggi pottery from North Korea.

1) Hoeryong Bukcheong Onggi or Bukcheong Basin (muldumeong)

Hoeryong pottery is completed with a streamlined body and the soft, subtle tones are beautiful.

Hoeryong onggi of the Five Northern Korean Provinces is a speciality of the Hamgyong province characterized by the modest quietude of the form which enhances its unique simple elegance. Produced in remote local kiln sites with not much exchange happening with the outside world, it seems Hoeryong pottery reflects the artistic vision of a potter who could freely unleash his creative expression without interference or restraint. It is made without artifice that can only serve beauty, because it is an object with no visual trickery that has no purpose other than for everyday use.

It is not an overstatement to say that the potter who made Hoeryong pottery communes with God through nature.

Hoeryong onggi takes its name from Hoeryong in North Hamgyong Province where it was made. In its long history on the Korean peninsula, Hoeryong onggi is the representative pottery manufactured in the northern region of the peninsula made of a mixture of clay and wood with excellent fire resistance. Onggi, our traditional earthenware that is part of our daily life evolved as new discoveries were made using soil and raw materials present in the region.

Hoeryong onggi is characterized by its deep beautiful color formation which was completed by using advanced techniques to create color derived from the trees and plants found in the surrounding nature without using artificial processes or metal oxides.

Hoeryong Bukcheong Onggi is another masterpiece of Hamgyeong Province Onggi that is unknown to the world.

It is said that the local people carried onggi on their heads and came to Seoul to sell water in Bukchon and Sajik-dong area. Hoeryong Bukcheong onggi that have survived in South Korea had spread through this process and these wares are all that remain. Another name for Bukcheong onggi is Bukcheong muldumeong (basin).

Currently in North Korea, Juel, Hamgyeongbuk Province,

situated near Gyeongseong is known to produce souvenir products for Chinese and Russian tourists such as tourist Hoeryong onggi and Bukcheong pottery. An appreciation of the beauty of Hoeryong pottery had developed in Japan around the time of Imjin War (invasion of Korea by Japan) which led to the transfer of glazing technology for Karatsu pottery, one of the three major types of pottery (Raku, Hagi, and Karatsu) that Japan takes great pride in.

2) Kaesong, Haeju Onggi

After the decline of Goryeo Dynasty, the people of Kaesong expanded their business through great strategies and played a pivotal role in inter-Korean trade. In the late Joseon Dynasty, merchants of Songdo were as wealthy as aristocrats. It is presumed that they made a separate order for well crafted onggi, rather than use white porcelain which reflected the aristocratic culture of the Joseon Dynasty. Among the onggi pottery made in Kaesong, there is an abundance of onggi fired with Seokganju mineral glaze which are distinguished by their beauty and high quality such as the wine bottle with long graceful neck, sinseollo pot, and incense burner.

Haeju pottery was made in luminous white porcelain decorated with azure blue achieving a finish of the highest form of beauty, which was also regarded as a symbol of the upper class.

Imported by Arab merchants in the 14th century, Persian cobalt was more expensive than gold. The cobalt blue pigment imported through China into Korea was reserved exclusively for the privileged class and used only for porcelain of superb quality. However, in the 19th century western artificial pigment was introduced in large quantities and popularized through mass production, and it began to be called yangcheong (western blue). Using this pigment the natural environment and characteristics of the Kanseo region were painted in minhwa style (folk painting), and the finished product was Haeju jar with blue decoration on the soft porcelain clay. The manufacturing process used for onggi in this period, even the forming and firing techniques was very similar to that used for oji ware.

Onggi from North Korea
Hoeryong Onggi, Haeju Onggi, Bukcheong Onggi

Hoeryong onggi, a North Korean pottery, has both high artistic and cultural value. The pottery produced in the regions of Woongjin, Yeonbaek, Kaesong, and Haeju can be considered to be of high quality. The few onggi wares the fleeing refugees brought with them during the Korean War exhibit the geographical qualities that represent the northern region characteristics and is the object of a study that should be sufficiently revisited. Bukcheong onggi is another famous Hamgyeongdo onggi that is unknown to the outside world.

Haeju Hangari

Haeju hangari spread to the northern region of Hansu and dominated the oji ware production regions, and was called the heretic of the Joseon ceramics. A jangdokdae with a collection of white hangari pots was a symbol of a wealthy family. The hangari pots radiated beauty especially through the depictions of fish, peony, pavilion, and sipjangsaeng scheme (ten longevity symbols) which were used indoors as storage jars for rice, honey, seasoning, and gyeongok-go (herbal medicine). The ones used to contain kimchi and sauces were stored outdoors.

The pottery may lack technical finesse, but exudes a quaint simple charm from which we can contemplate the potter's breath and focused concentration from the past. The sad reality is that due to lack of historical data and indifference, the authentic cultural expressions of onggi cannot come to light.

It is my hope to complete a dining table setting with healthy dishes by discovering the traditional sauces with truly beneficial properties based on meju made from Korean soybeans which are fermented with natural beneficial bacteria, and stored in the respiring onggi with high air permeability and great storage function.

During the Japanese colonial rule, in July 1937, the Japanese bacteriologists argued that the invention of "fermented soybeans" could reduce the economic burden on Joseon families, and by decree of the Japanese Government-General of Korea an order was issued to remove the jangdokdae from each household. In this manner, even the traditional Korean sauces were dismissed as mere entertainment objects, and the precious cultural food traditions on the Korean peninsula were in serious danger of being eradicated. In addition, the Japanese colonial rule obliterated our traditional fermentation technology.

As a countermeasure against these changes, based on the lessons learned from the history of traditional gayangju liquor, which was banned during the Japanese colonial period, we anticipate the development and educational support for small farms as well as omnidirectional research to take place in order to restore the traditional jang pastes to their authentic version.

Therefore, we look forward to Korea's fermented soybean products becoming a global player in the slow food movement.

Acknowledgements

In my opinion, onggi reflects the long history of the Korean people forming an ideal harmony of our own emotions and traditions, and through its solid weight and unique nature conveys a sense of completeness that cannot be replaced.

I attempted to write this book based on the understanding that I need to approach the respiring onggi from a new perspective, in a broad spatial and temporal context, from the long history of onggi that existed since ancient times to its widespread dispersal intended for household use.

Our respiring onggi is immersed in nature that offers a profound connection with the warmth of the soil, the nostalgic charm of days gone by, and vitality.

As I explored the techniques in onggi production, the respiring onggi made by human hand embraced me full of familiarity and comfort, and a sense of nostalgia of a grandmother from the past. It was nice to be freed from any kind of decorum or tension due to my insistent engagement with nature.

The respiring onggi has been in use by the Koreans before the Three Kingdoms Period (57 BCE – 668 CE) which has artistic value due to its ease of use and stylish appeal to this day. Although onggi was widely used in ordinary households until the 1970s, it is a great pity that it is gradually disappearing from our surroundings. For this reason, I am committed to raising awareness of the onggi's versatility which works well with just about anything and used for a variety of purposes. Except for the earthenware pots placed in jangdokdae most of the onggi pots can be seen today only in museums, and they have never been considered as cultural heritage properties worthy of state-designated "national treasures" or "treasures," and regarded as just one of the folk art material commonly found around us. Since there were also no institutions with formal programs or professors teaching onggi making, it was only possible to learn the craft through apprenticeship by visiting the old kiln sites or craftspeople in the region.

The walls of onggi have micro-pores enabling the traditional liquor to taste good. Compared to other pottery in terms of hardness and water absorption ability, the possibilities of onggi are limitless. Sourced directly from the earth, onggi is eco-friendly because it can return to nature when it is broken and discarded. My dream is that some day onggi will make a comeback as many people constantly discover the charm of onggi characterized by its humble yet chic form. The days when potters were looked down upon no longer exist and these days young students are coming to the workshop voluntarily to learn which is giving me great strength and hope.

It is said that the air holes which are the most significant quality of Korean onggi are not found in Chinese earthenware crocks. In 1996, master craftsman Hwang Chung-gil created a kimchi storage onggi which was designated as an important craft work of a "Master Hand" in 1998.

Hwang Jin-young, the son of Hwang Chung-gil, who grew up to his father constantly saying, "It is a pity there is no one who will inherit the skills," focused on the scientific study of pottery in college, and married a woman who majored in pottery. Now the husband and wife onggi duo is working on converting "the feelings and touch of Hwang's father" into scientific data. What is surprising is that the father's rich reservoir full of life experiences and his son's scientific analysis are almost identical.

Hwang Jin-young explained his work is about "finding an easier way of making onggi through objective analysis that shows the cumulative body of experiences handed down from the ancestors to my father was science," and expressed respect for his father's experience. He added that he wants to walk the path where the human hand and design converge.

"Grown-ups started this work to make a living, but I do it because I love the work. I want to pass this on to my son. I wonder will the child who was looking at the onggi made by his grandfather touch the soil and light the kiln…"

The path Hwang walks represents the great strength and hope he is giving to young people who want to be pioneers shaping the future of onggi. The government should nurture future talents and provide institutional support, such as designating Hwang as a living national treasure.

It is regrettable that onggi is being sold as a "valuable big jar" to foreigners who first recognized its splendor. I believe as the original custodians of onggi, even now by coming to recognize and protect its magnificence and preciousness we can show our patriotism.

The "respiring onggi" did not receive proper recognition despite being established as the most essential of necessities in our lives, and as a national vessel it needs to be proudly embraced with the philosophy that "what is most authentic Korean is what is most global" in order to be preserved for a long time as Korea's unique cultural legacy in the world. With this zealous tenacity I will be a friend to the "respiring onggi."

Since I decided to publish this book I have encountered various onggi pottery found on the Korean peninsula, including onggi of the Five Northern Korean Provinces which became more precious since it is now impossible to visit the regions due to the inter-Korean division. At the time I could feel the buried memories and longing in each pottery. And I realized this is a precious part of our culture, a history that has continued all the way from the past, and that we have lived a life of repeated mistakes that can never be fixed.

I hope by helping in a small way this book can deepen our understanding of why "respiring onggi" must be registered as UNESCO's Intangible Cultural Heritage.

There is now a global movement for food culture to return to naturalism. This means there is a growing interest in kimchi, the fermented food made in our respiring onggi. I think the registration of making and sharing kimchi as a UNESCO heritage was possible due to the onggi culture, which is based on the science of fermentation and has played a key role in maintaining the health of the nation providing the foundation for the global recognition of kimchi. In addition, the reason for the selection of Korean food kimchi as one of the world's five healthiest foods was based on the fact that it is rich in lactic acid bacteria and various vitamins.

The reason Korea is called the kingdom of fermented food is not only because of the production and consumption of a variety of fermented food, but also because of its outstanding technology in storing and preserving those foods, in other words, thanks to "respiring onggi."

> *Like clay in the hand of the potter.*
> *so are you in my hand, Israel.*
> - Jeremiah 18:6

Parable of the potter in Jeremiah 18:6 in the Old Testament. It means that everything is in the hands of God, and the moment it is in God's hands, it will be made into something amazing.

I would like to thank Professor Song Jaeseon, who taught us about the excellence of onggi in Korea, and to Professor Cho Jung-hyun, Department of Ceramics at Ewha Womans University, a ceramic artist who clarified the concept of onggi and let the world know about the great achievements of onggi, and also a great source of strength for writing this book. I am grateful to Jeong Hee-chang, CEO of Jang Seong-chang Art, who discovered the charm of onggi by creating the earthenware with its various advantages, and in particular, continuously developed onggi making to catch the attention of many people and draw them in, and voluntarily invited young students to the workshop so they could become the "great force" in keeping onggi culture alive. In addition, I have appreciated the help of Go Seung-gwang, director of Onggi Cultural Center, who owns several pieces of North Korean pottery and trained my eyes to see its artistry, and thanks to the residents and governors of the Five Northern Korean Provinces, I was able to prepare a little cornerstone of research materials. I am also grateful to the governors of the North and South Hamgyong Provinces, the North and South Provinces of Pyeongan, and the Hwanghae Provinces for their generous help and compassion.

This technology that had been severed after the Imjin War in 1592 was brought back by Choi Myeongjae in the 1920s and continues the link from the predecessors. Due to the severed diplomatic relations with North Korea as a result of the division of Korea, the Korean artists who studied in Japan are currently recreating and continuing the traditions of onggi making. And I congratulate Shin Han-kyun, a young potter in Busan, who recreated Hoeryong onggi after much trial and error.

I am deeply indebted to the first generation elderly refugees from Hoeryong-gun who gave me encouragement and willingly provided the authentic artifacts confirmed by the memories and testimonies of the people who actually used Hoeryong onggi. as well as the map depicting Hoeryong and helped me to identify the kiln sites near Hoeryong and the historic sites in the nearby area of Samhap where onggi was produced. I am immensely grateful to them for their hard work and dedication.

After graduating from the Department of Ceramics and Glass at Hongik University, Kim Yeon-soo, who was registered with the Korea Ceramic Foundation recognized for his youthful, vigorous career and his numerous exhibitions and awards as well as his accumulated experience at home and abroad, is an artist who has visited the United States as part of his artistic projects, including the MICA (Maryland Institute College of Art) and has a collection of various works from

Korea and overseas. Kim is inspiring hope to keep Korean onggi alive by promoting the style and beauty rooted in our culture.

Any shortcomings in my writing are my own responsibility.

I hope that you will find the reference list a useful guide.

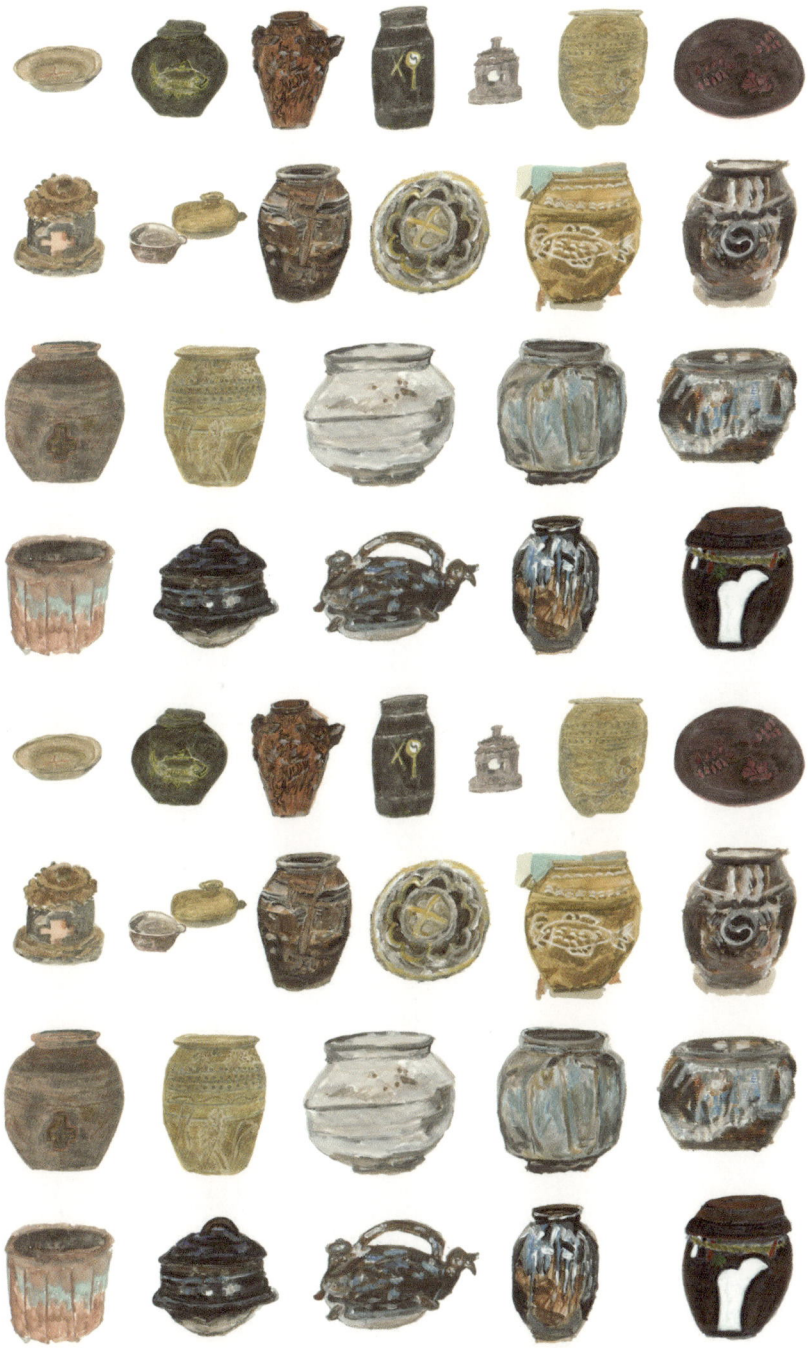

숨 쉬는 옹기,
그 멋에 끌리다

Respiring Onggi Object of Admiration

김덕신 그리고 쓰다
Written and illustrated by Kim Duk Shin